FEDERAL REPUBLIC OF YUGOSLAVIA

A Week of Terror in Drenica
Humanitarian Law Violations in Kosovo

Human Rights Watch
New York · Washington · London · Brussels

ISBN 1-56432-227-0
Library of Congress Catalog Card Number: 99-60896

Cover and internal photographs © Peter Bouckaert, 1999, for Human Rights Watch.

Addresses for Human Rights Watch:
350 Fifth Avenue, 34th Floor, New York, NY 10118-3299
Tel: (212) 290-4700, Fax: (212) 736-1300, E-mail: hrwnyc@hrw.org

1522 K Street, NW, #910, Washington, DC 20005-1202
Tel: (202) 371-6592, Fax: (202) 371-0124, E-mail: hrwdc@hrw.org

33 Islington High Street, N1 9LH London, UK
Tel: (171) 713-1995, Fax: (171) 713-1800, E-mail: hrwatchuk@gn.apc.org

15 Rue Van Campenhout, 1000 Brussels, Belgium
Tel: (2) 732-2009, Fax: (2) 732-0471, E-mail: hrwatcheu@gn.apc.org

Web Site Address: http://www.hrw.org
Gopher Address://gopher.humanrights.org:5000/11/int/Human Rights Watch
Listserv Address: To subscribe to the list, send an e-mail message to majordomo@igc.apc.org with "subscribe Human Rights Watch-news" in the body of the message (leave the subject blank).

HUMAN RIGHTS WATCH

Human Rights Watch conducts regular, systematic investigations of human rights abuses in some seventy countries around the world. Our reputation for timely, reliable disclosures has made us an essential source of information for those concerned with human rights. We address the human rights practices of governments of all political stripes, of all geopolitical alignments, and of all ethnic and religious persuasions. Human Rights Watch defends freedom of thought and expression, due process and equal protection of the law, and a vigorous civil society; we document and denounce murders, disappearances, torture, arbitrary imprisonment, discrimination, and other abuses of internationally recognized human rights. Our goal is to hold governments accountable if they transgress the rights of their people.

Human Rights Watch began in 1978 with the founding of its Europe and Central Asia division (then known as Helsinki Watch). Today, it also includes divisions covering Africa, the Americas, Asia, and the Middle East. In addition, it includes three thematic divisions on arms, children's rights, and women's rights. It maintains offices in New York, Washington, Los Angeles, London, Brussels, Moscow, Dushanbe, Rio de Janeiro, and Hong Kong. Human Rights Watch is an independent, nongovernmental organization, supported by contributions from private individuals and foundations worldwide. It accepts no government funds, directly or indirectly.

The staff includes Kenneth Roth, executive director; Michele Alexander, development director; Reed Brody, advocacy director; Carroll Bogert, communications director; Cynthia Brown, program director; Barbara Guglielmo, finance and administration director; Jeri Laber, special advisor; Lotte Leicht, Brussels office director; Patrick Minges, publications director; Susan Osnos, associate director; Jemera Rone, counsel; Wilder Tayler, general counsel; and Joanna Weschler, United Nations representative. Jonathan Fanton is the chair of the board. Robert L. Bernstein is the founding chair.

The regional directors of Human Rights Watch are Peter Takirambudde, Africa; José Miguel Vivanco, Americas; Sidney Jones, Asia; Holly Cartner, Europe and Central Asia; and Hanny Megally, Middle East and North Africa. The thematic division directors are Joost R. Hiltermann, arms; Lois Whitman, children's; and Regan Ralph, women's.

The members of the board of directors are Jonathan Fanton, chair; Lisa Anderson, Robert L. Bernstein, William Carmichael, Dorothy Cullman, Gina Despres, Irene Diamond, Adrian W. DeWind, Fiona Druckenmiller, Edith Everett, James C. Goodale, Vartan Gregorian, Alice H. Henkin, Stephen L. Kass, Marina Pinto Kaufman, Bruce Klatsky, Harold Hongju Koh, Alexander MacGregor, Josh Mailman, Samuel K. Murumba, Andrew Nathan, Jane Olson, Peter Osnos, Kathleen Peratis, Bruce Rabb, Sigrid Rausing, Anita Roddick, Orville Schell, Sid Sheinberg, Gary G. Sick, Malcolm Smith, Domna Stanton, and Maya Wiley. Robert L. Bernstein is the founding chair of Human Rights Watch.

ACKNOWLEDGMENTS

This report is based on extensive research conducted on three field missions to Kosovo between September and December 1998 by Fred Abrahams and Peter Bouckaert, researchers at Human Rights Watch. The report was written by Peter Bouckaert. Fred Abrahams contributed to certain sections and edited the report. The report was also edited by Holly Cartner, executive director of the Europe and Central Asia division, Jeri Laber, senior adviser to Human Rights Watch, and Wilder Tayler, general counsel of Human Rights Watch. Invaluable production assistance was provided by Patrick Minges, publications director at Human Rights Watch, and Alexandra Perina, Human Rights Watch associate.

Human Rights Watch would like to acknowledge and thank the many individuals whose contributions made this report possible, especially the human rights groups that are working in Yugoslavia under difficult conditions. Special thanks go to the victims and witnesses of abuses in Kosovo who provided testimony and information in the hope that the perpetrators of war crimes will be brought to justice.

TABLE OF CONTENTS

Kosovo

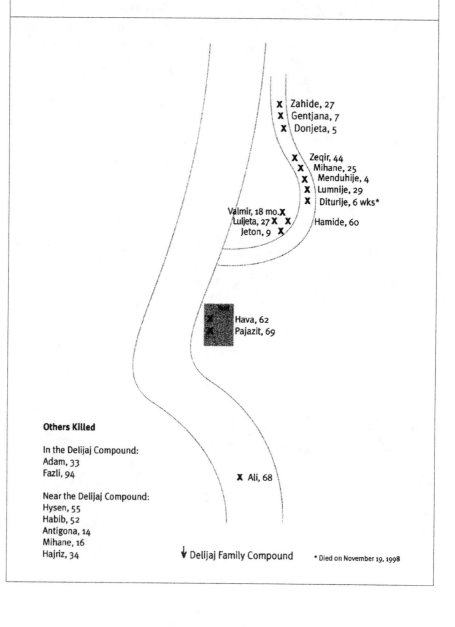

GORNJE OBRINJE
NEAR DELIJAJ FAMILY COMPOUND
SEPTEMBER 26, 1998

X Zahide, 27
X Gentjana, 7
X Donjeta, 5

X Zeqir, 44
X Mihane, 25
X Menduhije, 4
X Lumnije, 29
X Diturije, 6 wks*

Valmir, 18 mo. X
Luljeta, 27 X   X Hamide, 60
Jeton, 9 X

X Hava, 62
X Pajazit, 69

Others Killed

In the Delijaj Compound:
Adam, 33
Fazli, 94

Near the Delijaj Compound:
Hysen, 55
Habib, 52
Antigona, 14
Mihane, 16
Hajriz, 34

X Ali, 68

↓ Delijaj Family Compound   * Died on November 19, 1998

I. SUMMARY

This report documents serious violations of international humanitarian law committed by Serbian and Yugoslav government forces in Kosovo's Drenica region during the last week of September 1998. As Yugoslav President Slobodan Milošević wrapped up a summer-long offensive against the Kosovo Liberation Army (KLA), special forces of the Serbian police (MUP) and Yugoslav Army (VJ) committed summary executions, indiscriminately attacked civilians, and systematically destroyed civilian property, all of which are violations of the rules of war and can be prosecuted by the International War Crimes Tribunal for the Former Yugoslavia (ICTY). These atrocities took place in the face of United Nations Security Council Resolution 1199, passed on September 23, 1998, which demanded an immediate cessation of all actions by the Yugoslav and Serbian security forces against civilians.

The war crimes documented in this report are neither the first nor the last committed by the government in the Yugoslav conflict. Most recently, on January 15, 1991, government forces killed forty-five ethnic Albanian civilians in the village of Račak, which has sparked the most recent round of diplomatic engagement (*see* Appendix A). The Kosovo Liberation Army has also committed serious abuses, including the taking of hostages and extrajudicial executions, which have been documented in previous Human Rights Watch reports and will continue to be the subject of investigation. Under no circumstances, however, can the Yugoslav government use abuses by the KLA as justification for committing abuses against ethnic Albanian civilians.

As the recent massacre in Račak show, President Milošević and his military planners believe they can continue their abusive campaign with impunity. This disturbing pattern of abuse can only be stopped by an unequivocal message from the international community that such blatant disregard for the most basic principles of humanity is unacceptable, and that the perpetrators of these abuses will be brought to justice. Any negotiations about the future status of Kosovo must include provisions to hold political leaders and members of the security forces accountable for human rights and humanitarian law violations during the conflict.

Human Rights Watch researchers were in Kosovo at the time the abuses documented in this report were committed and conducted two additional research missions to Kosovo, in November and December 1998, to document the crimes that took place in Drenica.

The worst incident documented in this report took place in late September 1998 at the Delijaj family compound in Gornje Obrinje, a village where there had been intense fighting between government forces and the KLA that left at least

1

fourteen policemen dead. Special police forces retaliated by killing twenty-one members of the Delijaj family, all of them civilians, on the afternoon of Saturday, September 26. Fourteen people were killed in a nearby forest where they were hiding from government shelling, six of them women between the ages of twenty-five and sixty-two. Five of the victims were children between eighteen months and nine years of age. Of the three men killed in the forest, two were over sixty years old.

Human Rights Watch visited the scene on September 29 while the bodies were being carried out of the forest for burial. All fourteen victims were wearing civilian clothing; most appeared to have been shot in the head at close range, and several of the bodies had been mutilated. In one case, the leg of sixty-two-year-old Hava Delijaj was cut off below the knee save for some skin.

In addition to the fourteen persons killed in the forest, seven other members of the Delijaj family were killed by government forces in and around the family compound. The ninety-four-year-old family patriarch Fazli Delijaj, an invalid, was found burned to death in his burned-out home. Habib and Hysen Delijaj were summarily executed by Serbian police in front of Hysen's wife and children. Adem Delijaj was found shot to death near his home in the family compound. Over the next few weeks, the decomposed bodies of two girls, Antigona and Mihane Delijaj, and of Hajriz Delijaj, were found in the general area of the massacre. One man, Sherif Delijaj, remains missing to this day.

After the forest massacre, Serbian special police forces arrived at the nearby Hysenaj family compound in Gornje Obrinje, together with four young Delijaj children whom they had apparently captured in the forest. The children were handed over to an elderly woman, Shehide Hysenaj, who then witnessed the police interrogate and beat a husband and wife before executing them with an axe. After the police left, Shehide found the body of her elderly husband near their home with a gun shot wound to his head. Human Rights Watch saw the bodies of these three persons three days after their deaths, and found the wounds on their bodies consistent with the testimony given by Shehide.

On September 27, the police also rounded up the civilians hiding in the forest near the Hysenaj compound, selected out twenty-two men, and drove them to the nearby village of Likovac, where the government forces were temporarily based. On the way, the men were repeatedly beaten by police. When they reached Likovac, a policeman walked up to the tractor, grabbed sixteen-year-old Driton Hysenaj by the hair, and slit his throat. The remaining twenty-one men were then driven to Glogovac police station, where they joined hundreds of other ethnic Albanian men who had been taken from their hiding places in the forests around Glogovac. The detainees were subjected to three days of physical abuse before being released. Several of the detainees were taken away and remain missing to this day.

On September 26, Serbian police also rounded up a group of several thousand civilians who had fled the shelling in Golubovac, a village just kilometers away from Gornje Obrinje. Fourteen men were ultimately selected out, interrogated, physically abused for several hours, and ultimately executed. The men were first sprayed with bullets from a short distance, then a police officer walked among the men, kicking them and shooting again at anyone who showed signs of life. One of the fourteen men miraculously survived by feigning death, and gave a detailed and damning testimony of the executions to Human Rights Watch, clearly holding the Serbian special police responsible. Several other witnesses corroborated his account of the day's events. Another villager, Ramadan Hoxha, was later found shot and burned in the forest outside Golubovac just meters away from where the police had encamped. All of the victims were male civilians.

The most common crime throughout Kosovo, and in Drenica specifically, has been the government's systematic destruction of civilian property, which presents further evidence of a military campaign against civilians in clear violation of the laws of war. Throughout Kosovo, the Yugoslav Army has shelled villages from a distance, and the Serbian police have followed by looting and burning. Water wells in some villages have been rendered useless through intentional contamination, and livestock have been shot. According to a recent UNHCR-sponsored assessment, 28 percent of all homes in the 210 Kosovo villages affected by the conflict have been completely destroyed.

The experiencě of the village of Pločica in Drenica, visited by Human Rights Watch on September 26 while the offensive was continuing, is typical. The villagers fled after they heard shelling and saw the police approaching, and returned the next day to find most of their village compound burned to the ground. Human Rights Watch did not find a single shell casing or any other evidence of fighting in Pločica, or signs that the KLA had used the village as a base. The evidence was clear: like many other villages, an abandoned Pločica had been systematically looted, trashed, and burned by the police.

Virtually all relevant governments and international organizations responded to the abuses in Drenica with outrage; governments threatened serious action, including possible air strikes by NATO. But, as with every other atrocity thus far in the Kosovo conflict, the international community did not back its words with serious preventative measures to discourage such atrocities from taking place again.

Although witnesses reported seeing forces of the Yugoslav Army, special police forces and special anti-terrorist forces (Specijalna Antiteroristicka Jedinica, or SAJ), both under the Ministry of the Interior, as well as the special forces unit (Jedinica za Specijalne Operacije, or JSO) commanded by Franko "Frenki" Simatovic and also under the Ministry of Interior, at the site of the atrocities documented in this report, the precise units of these forces that were responsible for the atrocities have not yet been identified. This information is clearly available to the Yugoslav authorities, who have publicly stated that its forces were in regular contact with their superiors.

Those who perpetrated crimes against ethnic Albanian civilians of Kosovo as well as those who planned them, encouraged them, tolerated or acquiesced to these crimes, must be held accountable for their intentional disregard for the laws of war. But the Yugoslav authorities, themselves deeply implicated and ultimately responsible for the abuses in Kosovo, are preventing the International War Crimes Tribunal for the Former Yugoslavia from effectively carrying out its investigations. The international community must apply the necessary pressure to ensure that the tribunal can investigate and prosecute the individuals responsible for these atrocities. The issue of accountability must be moved to center stage, in order to send the uncompromising message that brutal abuses against civilians will not be tolerated.

II. RECOMMENDATIONS

To the Yugoslav Government:
Compliance With International Humanitarian Law

- Put an end to summary executions. Investigate and prosecute those responsible for carrying out those acts;

- Stop the disproportionate use of force against the civilian population and the targeting of civilians for attacks during military and police operations; take all necessary steps to protect civilian populations from the effects of military and police operations;

- Stop the systematic destruction of civilian property. This includes the burning, pillage, and destruction of homes and food supplies, the burning and looting of crops and fodder, pollution of water sources, and the killing of livestock. The destruction of civilian objects constitutes a serious violation of the laws of war, and the perpetrators of such abuses should be prosecuted;

- Withdraw immediately from the Kosovo region all Serbian and Yugoslav forces and any paramilitary units that have or are suspected of having perpetrated human rights or humanitarian law violations; and

- Conduct an investigation in full cooperation with the ICTY, including any requests to defer prosecutions to the ICTY, and hold accountable those members of the police and security forces found responsible for violations of human rights and humanitarian law, including the summary executions of civilians at Gornje Obrinje and Golubovac. Such investigations should not serve as a cover to intimidate witnesses or to destroy relevant evidence.

Cooperation with the International Criminal Tribunal for the Former Yugoslavia (ICTY)

Cooperate fully with the ICTY in its efforts to investigate alleged violations of international humanitarian law on both sides in Kosovo. In particular:

- Adopt the measures necessary under Yugoslav law to implement the provisions of Security Council Resolution 827 and the statutes of the ICTY;

- Recognize the right of the ICTY to investigate all war crimes committed in the territory of the former Yugoslavia, including the area of Kosovo, as stated in U.N. Security Council Resolution 827 (1993), and repeatedly reaffirmed with particular reference to the Kosovo crisis in U.N. Security Council Resolutions 1160, 1199, and 1207;

- Immediately and unconditionally grant visas to all members of the ICTY investigative team, including members of the ICTY prosecutor's office and any independent experts working in conjunction with the ICTY;

- Allow the ICTY investigators full and unimpeded access to the full territory of the Federal Republic of Yugoslavia, including all areas of Kosovo;

- Recognize the authority of the ICTY to interview any witnesses and gather evidence of war crimes, including physical and forensic evidence;

- Assist the ICTY by making available relevant evidence and information about troop presence and command structures of the Yugoslav Army, Serbian police, and any other police or security unit that operated in Kosovo during the period of armed conflict, as well as such information regarding the police;

- Cooperate with the ICTY by locating and arresting any person under indictment by the ICTY.

Access for the OSCE, Human Rights and Humanitarian Organizations, and Media

- Guarantee safe passage and unencumbered access for humanitarian aid delivery and distribution;

- Provide unrestricted access for the U.N. Special Rapporteur on Human Rights in the Former Yugoslavia to investigate violations of humanitarian law and human rights by both sides in the Kosovo region;

- Grant independent human rights monitors immediate, full, and unfettered access to the Kosovo region in order to investigate allegations of humanitarian and human rights abuses. Grant independent human rights monitors the necessary visas to enable them to carry out their investigative work in the Kosovo region;

- Re-admit the Organization for Security and Cooperation in Europe's (OSCE's) long-term monitoring mission to the Federal Republic of Yugoslavia;

- Provide immediate and unimpeded access for teams of forensic experts to carry out investigations into allegations of human rights and humanitarian law violations in Kosovo;

- Allow full and unimpeded access to local and foreign journalists covering the conflict in Kosovo.

Treatment of and Access to Detainees

- End the widespread physical abuse and torture of persons in the custody of Yugoslav authorities, and stop the practice of arbitrarily arresting ethnic Albanian civilians during military and police operations;

- Fully disclose the names of all persons currently detained in the course of the conflict, their ages, the circumstances of their arrest, their current place of detention, the status of their prosecution or investigation, and any other relevant details. Investigate and clarify the whereabouts and fate of all persons believed to be in the custody of the authorities who remain unaccounted for;

- Maintain up-to-date registers of all detainees in every place of detention, locally and centrally; this information should be made available to relatives, lawyers and others;

- Allow the International Committee of the Red Cross (ICRC) unhindered, ongoing, and complete access to all detainees, including those who are being investigated but have not yet been charged with a crime;

- Allow diplomatic and independent monitors regular and unhindered access to persons in detention and to places of detention, in order to ensure that the treatment of detainees and conditions of detention are consistent with international obligations;

- Guarantee that detainees have regular access to their lawyers and family members, that they are able to meet with their lawyers in private, and that they have adequate time to prepare their defense;

- Conduct an investigation into the allegations of widespread torture and ill-treatment in detention. Those found responsible for such abuse should be held accountable before the law;

- Accord due process to all persons detained and/or accused of crimes, including ethnic Albanians accused of "violating the territorial integrity of Yugoslavia" or "terrorist" activities; and

- Drop all charges against and release from detention those who have been indicted for the peaceful expression of opinion or for membership in a group that has only performed acts which, under international human rights law, may not be criminalized, such as peaceful criticism of the government; and refrain from making arrests on such grounds.

To the Kosovo Liberation Army (KLA):

Because the fighting in Kosovo is an internal armed conflict covered by international humanitarian law, both government forces and the KLA are obliged to respect, at a minimum, the provisions of Common Article 3 of the Geneva Conventions, which require that civilians and other protected persons be treated humanely, with specific prohibitions on murder, torture, or cruel, humiliating or degrading treatment. Human Rights Watch, therefore, calls on the KLA to:

- Release all civilians in detention, refrain from attacks on members of the civilian population and from using any detainees or civilians as hostages, and treat humanely Serbian soldiers or policemen in custody;

- Condemn hostage-taking and the ill-treatment of civilians or others placed hors de combat and renounce such tactics;

- Impose a code of military conduct that punishes KLA hostage-taking, using humans as shields, and other conduct prohibited by international humanitarian law; take steps to inform troops of binding rules that violators among KLA troops will be held accountable;

- Bring to justice commanders and troops guilty of these violations in conformity with international standards of due process;

- Grant humanitarian organizations full and ongoing access to the conflict zone under KLA control and to people in KLA detention;

- Allow full and unconditional access to ICTY investigators, KVM verifiers, independent human rights investigators, diplomatic monitors, humanitarian workers, and the press to all areas under KLA control; and

- Cooperate fully with the ICTY and independent human rights investigators in bringing the perpetrators of human rights abuses and violations of international humanitarian law to justice.

To the International Community:
- Ensure that any negotiations about the future status of Kosovo do not serve as a mechanism to further impunity in the Federal Republic of Yugoslavia. Negotiated solutions must include provisions to hold political leaders and members of the security forces accountable for human rights abuses and violations of international humanitarian law committed during the Kosovo conflict;

Preventing Further Humanitarian Law Violations
- Respond to atrocities committed against civilians with decisive and immediate action;

- Insist that the conditions set forth in the Contact Group statement of March 9 and in the Holbrooke-Milošević Agreement of October 1998 are met by the Yugoslav government, and immediately respond to any violations of these agreements;

Supporting the work of the ICTY
- Put the issue of compliance with the mandate of the ICTY on the top of the international agenda, and in all interactions with the Yugoslav authorities insist on full cooperation with the ICTY;

- Insist that ICTY investigators and representatives be allowed to conduct investigations, including forensic investigations, in Kosovo with unimpeded access to all sites and witnesses. Immediately protest any

Yugoslav government actions which impede or attempt to interfere in the work of the ICTY;

• Guarantee ongoing financial and political support to ensure that the ICTY can undertake timely and thorough investigations into allegations of humanitarian law violations in Kosovo;

• Assist the ICTY in identifying important witnesses and evidence, and work closely with the ICTY in securing evidence and ensuring the protection of important witnesses;

• Provide the ICTY with any intelligence information obtained that relates to the commission of war crimes, including the identification of specific units engaged in operations in areas in which abuses occur, and convey relevant satellite intelligence information to the ICTY;

• Attach humanitarian law and human rights experts to the Kosovo Verification Mission (KVM), and ensure that any information gathered by these experts is shared with the ICTY;

• Ensure that all evidence relating to Slobodan Milosovic's and other political leaders' responsibility for war crimes in Kosovo, as well as in Bosnia and Hercegovina and Croatia, is turned over to the ICTY for investigation;

• Send a clear message that war crimes, crimes against humanity, and acts of genocide will not be tolerated by arresting those already indicted by the ICTY for atrocities committed during the wars in Bosnia and Croatia; and

• Raise awareness about the mandate and work of the ICTY and the obligations created by international humanitarian law through a public education campaign in both the Serbian and Albanian languages.

To the United Nations:
To the Security Council
The ongoing conflict in Kosovo remains a threat to regional stability and security, and the absence of a political solution to the conflict could lead to a

renewed escalation with widespread atrocities. Human Rights Watch therefore calls on the United Nations Security Council to:

- Ensure the implementation of Security Council Resolutions 1160, 1199 and 1207, which called for, among other things, an immediate cessation of hostilities and for the president of the Federal Republic of Yugoslavia to implement his own commitments from the June 16 joint statement with the president of the Russian Federation not to carry out any repressive actions against the peaceful population, to facilitate refugee return, and to cooperate with the ICTY;

- Call on the government of Slobodan Milošević to invite the U.N. Special Rapporteur on Extrajudicial, Summary and Arbitrary Executions, the U.N. Working Group on Arbitrary Detentions, and the U.N. Working Group on Enforced or Involuntary Disappearances urgently to conduct an investigation in Kosovo and to report back to the Security Council;

- Facilitate and encourage the work of the ICTY to investigate violations of international humanitarian law in Kosovo and guarantee ongoing financial and political support to ensure that the ICTY can undertake the necessary investigations; and

- Urge the Yugoslav government to cooperate with the ICTY, to adopt measures necessary under Yugoslav law to implement the provisions of Security Council Resolution 827 and the statutes of the tribunal, to transfer to the ICTY's custody those indicted persons on Yugoslav territory, and to facilitate an independent investigation of allegations of war crimes in Kosovo.

To the Commission on Human Rights
- Condemn the serious abuses committed in Kosovo and renew the mandate of the commission's special rapporteur on human rights in the former Yugoslavia to vigorously monitor human rights conditions throughout the conflict-affected region.

To the Special Rapporteur on Human Rights in the Former Yugoslavia
- Investigate and condemn violations of international human rights and humanitarian law committed in the Federal Republic of Yugoslavia and

communicate unequivocally to the parties to the conflict that there can be no justification, under international law, for such abuses.

To the High Commissioner on Human Rights

- Maintain a substantial staff in Kosovo to monitor abuses of human rights and violations of international humanitarian law; and

- Use your authority to encourage U.N. treaty bodies and mechanisms to be engaged in Kosovo and to facilitate access for these bodies and mechanisms to Kosovo.

To the International Criminal Tribunal for Yugoslavia

- Continue to seek to dispatch a high-level delegation, including Chief Prosecutor Louise Arbour, to Belgrade and Priština to put both sides on notice of the ICTY's mandate and the likely repercussions of international humanitarian law violations;

- Intensify efforts to investigate atrocities committed in Kosovo in a timely manner, including by dispatching teams of investigators to Kosovo, as well as to refugee-receiving areas, to interview victims and witnesses to atrocities and to gather relevant physical evidence and by coordinating the ICTY investigation with other international actors currently enjoying access to the conflict area;

- Ensure that witnesses, particularly those still based in Kosovo, are provided with adequate protection; and

- Engage in a public education campaign in Kosovo, aimed at informing parties to the conflict about their obligations under international humanitarian law and ensuring that civilians are aware of the work of the ICTY and ways to contact the ICTY with relevant information.

To the Organization for Security and Cooperation in Europe:

Human Rights Watch believes that in order to help prevent a recurrence of the type of abuses described in this report and to be effective in the implementation of its mandate, the OSCE Kosovo Verification Mission (KVM) must maintain a strong human rights orientation in its work. The human rights mandate of the OSCE KVM mission should empower and oblige the mission to:

Freely monitor and investigate human rights abuses
- Receive complaints of human rights abuses from any person or group in Kosovo;

- Travel freely and visit any site, including any suspected or known place of detention;

- Interview people freely and in private, including detainees who have not yet been charged with a crime;

Monitor, report, and publicize abuses committed by the security forces
- Monitor the behavior of the Serbian police and Yugoslav army and investigate incidents of harassment or violence against the civilian population; raise cases of abuse with the appropriate authorities; recommend corrective action, including dismissal or prosecution; and publicize the abuses, particularly in cases where the authorities fail to take appropriate corrective action;

Monitor, report, and publicize KLA abuses
- Monitor and investigate any harassment or abuse by the Kosovo Liberation Army against ethnic Albanians, Serbs, and others; report those abuses to the KLA and the Yugoslav authorities; recommend accountability or other corrective action in conformity with international standards; and publicize the abuses, particularly where the KLA or Yugoslav authorities fail to take appropriate action;

Monitor, report, and publicize conditions of detention
- In cooperation with ICRC, monitor the treatment of those in detention through regular visits to prisons, police stations, and suspected places of detention, including those located outside of Kosovo but holding persons detained in connection with the conflict; interview detainees, freely and in private, including those who have not yet been charged with a crime; raise objections with the authorities when access to detention facilities is denied or conditions deviate from international standards; recommend corrective action, including dismissal or prosecution; and publicize those conditions when the authorities fail to take corrective action, including the prosecution of responsible officials;

Monitor, report, and publicize conduct of trials
- Observe trials, especially those of ethnic Albanians accused of "terrorism" or other crimes related to state security; raise objections with the authorities when access to trials is denied and when procedural irregularities are identified; recommend remedial measures; and publicize procedural violations, particularly when the authorities fail to take remedial action;

Monitor, report, and publicize conditions for return of displaced persons
- Monitor and investigate obstacles to the right of return for the estimated 250,000 internally displaced persons in Kosovo; bring those obstacles to the attention of the authorities; recommend remedial measures; and publicize the problem, particularly when the authorities fail to remedy it;

Monitor, report, and publicize restrictions on the media
- Monitor and investigate restrictions on freedom of the press in Serbia, both on the Albanian- and Serbian-language media; publicize deficiencies in freedom of expression and recommend needed reform to the authorities;

Work with local and international human rights organizations
- Maintain close contact with local and international human rights organizations working in Kosovo and develop procedures for regular consultation and information sharing;

Cooperate with the ICTY
- Cooperate fully with the International Criminal Tribunal for the Former Yugoslavia by identifying possible witnesses and evidence of violations of international humanitarian law. To facilitate this cooperation, mission members should be briefed on the specific evidentiary needs of the ICTY and instructed to forward relevant information;

Contribute to human rights institution building
- Lead or participate in efforts to assist in the development of national institutions—both governmental and nongovernmental—which can protect and promote human rights after the international monitoring has ended; and

Vet the police force for human right abusers

- As part of police force development as envisioned by the October agreement between FRY and the OSCE establishing the KVM mandate, ensure that police officers responsible for war crimes or other serious human rights violations are not allowed to serve in any capacity in law enforcement. For purposes of the vetting of police officers, the OSCE should seek information regarding individual police officers' human rights records from the ICTY, local and international human rights groups, and the public, as well as from the OSCE's own human rights monitors.

In conclusion, Human Rights Watch notes that the OSCE should not limit its engagement in FRY to the verification mission. First, the new OSCE mission to Kosovo should not be considered a replacement for the long-term, Yugoslav-wide OSCE mission that was expelled from the country in 1992. Such a mission to monitor human rights conditions throughout Yugoslavia is essential to any viable long-term political solution in FRY and should remain a central demand of the international community. Second, while recognizing limitations on his mandate, Human Rights Watch believes that the OSCE High Commissioner on National Minorities might play an important role in Kosovo, providing an early warning mechanism for possible renewed violence stemming from abuses committed against Albanians, Serbs or other minorities resident in the region. Finally, the OSCE should support recent efforts of its Representative on Freedom of the Media to address the serious violations of free expression that undermine prospects for any lasting political solution in FRY.

III. GORNJE OBRINJE: MASSACRE IN THE FOREST

The Fighting at Gornje Obrinje

In mid-July, 1998, the Yugoslav Army and Serbian police began a major offensive against the KLA, which had assumed loose control of an estimated one-third of Kosovo. The offensive, which involved heavy artillery, tanks, and occasional air power, was highly effective in driving the KLA from most of its established positions into pockets in the mountains and woods.

In the end, however, very few KLA fighters were killed or captured. The brunt of the suffering was borne by ethnic Albanian civilians who lived in the areas of conflict. More than two hundred villages were destroyed and at least 300,000 people were internally displaced. Most of the estimated 2,000 people killed through September were civilians.

The dangers faced by civilians in the Kosovo conflict were articulated by the International Committee of the Red Cross (ICRC), in a public statement issued in September:

> At this very moment, as has been the case for several weeks now, tens of thousands of civilians are caught up in a devastating cycle of attacks and displacements. They are exposed to violence, including threats to their lives, destruction of their homes, separation from their families, and abductions. Thousands of them have nowhere left to go and no one to turn to for protection.
>
> From a humanitarian perspective, it has become apparent that civilian casualties are not simply what has become known as "collateral damage." In Kosovo, civilians have become the main victims—if not the actual targets—of the fighting.[1]

By mid-September, international pressure was building on Milošević to halt the offensive. By that time, however, the government had virtually succeeded in destroying all the towns and settlements in which the KLA was present, driving the fighters into the woods. The campaign of destruction remained unfinished in one important area: central Drenica, where some of the most intense fighting between the KLA and government forces had taken place.

---

[1]International Committee of the Red Cross statement on Kosovo, September 1998.

16

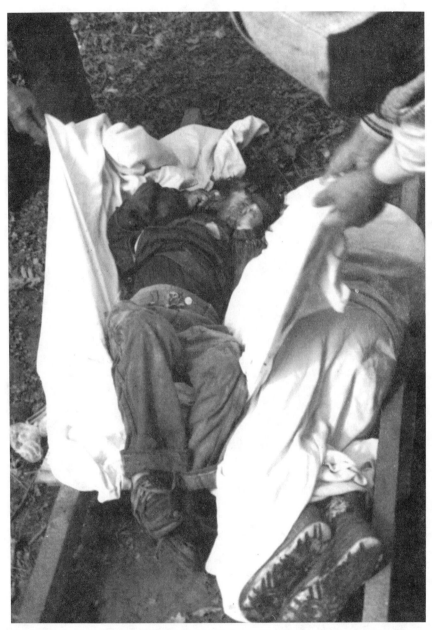

The bodies of Donjeta and Gentjana Delijaj, age five and seven respectively, being carried out of the forest in preparation for burial. © 1999 Human Rights Watch.

A member of the Delijaj family in despair after viewing the remains of fourteen family members in the forest. September 29, 1998. © 1999 Human Rights Watch.

The burial of eighteen members of the Delijaj family at Gornje Obrinje on September 29, 1998. Three additional family members were found dead over the next weeks, bringing the total number of persons killed at the compound to twenty-one. © 1999 Human Rights Watch.

A member of the Delijaj family standing outside a destroyed home in Gornje Obrinje. November 1998. © 1999 Human Rights Watch.

There is little doubt that the final days of the offensive were a carefully calculated gamble. President Milosovic and his military planners knew that they had little time left to complete their objectives in Kosovo and then avert a Western military response by ordering a rapid and dramatic pull-back of forces. The underlying motives for the brutality of the Yugoslav offensive remain difficult to discern—the Yugoslav security forces certainly succeeded in sending a message to ethnic Albanians in Kosovo that brutal repression would follow any attempts to assert ethnic Albanian control in Kosovo.

The village of Gornje Obrinje is located in Drenica's Glogovac municipality. The 500-year-old village has approximately 300 houses divided up among several large family compounds separated by fields and woods, including the family compounds of the Delijaj and Hysenaj families where many of the atrocities discussed in this report took place. Three kilometers to the north is the hilltop village of Likovac, which served as a regional KLA headquarters prior to the Yugoslav offensive and was recaptured by Yugoslav forces around September 13.[2]

During the month of September, government forces mounted an offensive in the Drenica region, attempting to dislodge the KLA from its Drenica stronghold. The police and army attacked from the direction of the town of Klina, southwest of Glogovac, as well as from the Čičavica mountains in the east, and effectively surrounded KLA forces in the hilly Obrinje region. According to Naim Maloku, a senior commander of the KLA and a former Yugoslav Army officer interviewed by the *New York Times*, the Yugoslav forces faced stiff resistance from the KLA in the Likovac-Obrinje area:

> [T]he guerrillas, caught in a Serbian pincer movement, had decided to fight rather than surrender. The fighting—sometimes house to house, even room to room—took an unusually heavy toll among the Serbs ... [T]he guerrillas fought, using land mines and rocket-propelled grenades. Mr. Maloku said that he knew from a report made by rebel headquarters that at least 47 Serbian soldiers and police officers were killed in the fighting between

---

[2]Jane Perlez, "Ethnic Albanians Recount Massacre of a Family in Kosovo," *New York Times*, November 15, 1998.

[Obrinje] and Bajinca, three miles east. "We took weapons from 47 Serbs," he said.[3]

After taking Likovac, the government forces moved on to Obrinje. According to Zejnije ("Zora") Delijaj, who was in Gornje Obrinje with her family at the beginning of the offensive, government forces began shelling the Delijaj compound from the direction of Likovac at around 8 a.m. on Friday, September 26, with various types of artillery and mortars.[4] Most of the inhabitants of the compound fled to the forest to escape the shelling. Bashkim Delijaj, twenty-one, was one of the only civilians who remained behind in the Delijaj compound at the time of the attack in order to care for his elderly father, the ninety-four-year-old Fazli, who was an invalid. Bashkim described to Human Rights Watch how the attack continued on Saturday morning:

> When it got dark on Friday, the police returned to Likovac. During the night, they continued shelling. Around 7 a.m. the next day, they started shelling again. Half of the tank convoy based in Likovac, about sixty-eight tanks, started moving toward the Delijaj compound. They were firing ground-to-ground missiles at us from the tanks. The infantry was moving behind the tanks; many of them had beards. I was staying with my father who was handicapped and needed food and water. We were smoking a cigarette when a grenade fell on the roof.

> I jumped out of the second floor of the house and ran toward the gate. I was looking through a hole in the gate and saw the army was burning the neighborhood. I saw soldiers coming from about thirty meters away. They had [brown] army uniforms, and many of them had either huge knives or small axes, I couldn't see clearly. I started fleeing toward the Berdolak neighborhood.[5]

For the next several days, the Yugoslav forces remained in effective control of the Obrinje area, and carried out the abuses described in this report.

---

[3]Ibid.

[4]Human Rights Watch interview with Zejnije Delijaj, Mitrovica, November 11, 1998.

[5]Human Rights Watch interview with Bashkim Delijaj, Priština, November 11, 1998.

Because most villagers fled the oncoming offensive, it is difficult to identify precisely which government forces participated in the abuses. However, those present in the area at the time identified at least three types of forces: the Serbian special police under the jurisdiction of the Ministry of Interior (MUP), distinguished by their blue camouflage uniforms; the special anti-terrorist force (SAJ), also under the control of the Ministry of Interior, distinguished by their darker brown camouflage uniforms; and contingents of the Yugoslav Army (VJ), recognizable from their green uniforms and the presence of tanks and other heavy artillery. According to a senior KLA commander for Drenica interviewed by Human Rights Watch at the funeral of Driton Hysenaj (see below), the special forces unit (Jedinica za Specijalne Operacije, or JSO) headed by Franko "Frenki" Simatovic and popularly known as "Frenki's boys," were also present during the fighting in the Obrinje area. The JSO wear irregular uniforms, often appearing in the uniforms of other military or police units, and are reputed to carry large knives, something several witnesses mentioned seeing near Obrinje. The JSO have a reputation for ruthlessness. In the words of a Serbian policeman who spent six months in Kosovo near Deçan, interviewed by Human Rights Watch in Belgrade, "Frenki's boys kill everything. Believe me, you do no want to see them."[6]

On September 26, Human Rights Watch observed a convoy of forty-seven heavily armored military vehicles and sixteen supply or support vehicles leaving Drenica around the village of Mlečane, a few miles west of Glogovac. The convoy included numerous tanks, heavy artillery, anti-aircraft guns, pontoon bridges, and armored personnel carriers.

According to the Priština Media Center, a media center with close ties to the Serbian government, at least seven policemen died in the Obrinje area on September 25, 1998, the day prior to the massacre of the Delijaj family and the summary executions at nearby Golubovac. Five police reservists were also killed near Likovac when their vehicle hit an anti-tank land mine that was probably placed by the KLA. The names of the police reservists killed are:[7]

- Goran Zivadinović, born in 1969, from Soko Banja;
- Slavomir Bojanić, born in 1970, from Priboj;
- Ognjen Petrović, born in 1975, from Novi Sad;

---

[6]Human Rights Watch interview with J.J., Belgrade, November 2, 1998. The policeman confirmed the conclusion of Human Rights Watch that the JSO had engaged in "sweep up" operations in the Deçan area.

[7]Media Centar Priština Press Release, September 26,1998, 13:00 hrs.

- Dragoslav Tadić, born in 1962, from Vrbas;
- Aleksandar Pantović, born in 1973, from Vrbas.

The Media Center further reported that two policemen were killed on September 25 "at about 2 p.m. by a heavily armed group of Albanians nearby Donje Obrinje village."[8] They were:

- Miroslav Slović, born in 1974, from Zubin Potok;
- Rajko Radovanović, born in 1973, from Srbica.

On September 27, 1998, the day after the Obrinje massacre but before the site had been discovered, the Priština Media Center put out the following statement that three Serbian policemen had been killed in the Obrinje area on September 26, and that the police had succeeded in capturing the villages of Gornje and Donje Obrinje:

> Three [Serbian] policemen were killed in an attack by Albanian
> extremists near the village of Donje Obrinje, west of Glogovac,
> at around 15:30 yesterday. The three policemen killed, who
> came from the town of Kruševac were Veljko Mijković
> [probably Miljković] (1968), Sreten Milić (1970) and Ljubomir
> Ljumirović [probably Ljumbomirović] (1966). ... According to
> Glogovac municipal authorities, the police captured Albanian
> extremist strongholds in the villages of Gornje and Donje
> Obrinje, as well as the wider area of Glogovac. During the
> operation against the terrorist stronghold in the area, at least ten
> members of the secessionist Kosovo Liberation Army were
> killed, the municipal authorities reported.[9]

On September 26, Human Rights Watch researchers observed a Yugoslav army red cross helicopter fly over the village of Pločica in the direction of Gornje Obrinje, which could be seen burning in the distance, and return approximately twenty minutes later.

---

[8]Media Centar Priština Press Release, September 26, 1998, 13:00 hrs. Human Rights Watch investigations have established that the killed men were probably not from the exact towns mentioned in the release, but rather from villages in the environs.

[9]Media Centar Priština Press Release, September 27, 1998, 14:00 hrs. The corrected spellings are based on additional research by Human Rights Watch

Yugoslav authorities certainly are able to identify the police and army units responsible for the atrocities documented in this report. While denying the police were responsible for the massacres, spokesman for the Ministry of Interior, police colonel Božidar Filić, confirmed that "police units which took part in breaking up terrorist bands were under the direct command of their superior officers who submitted regular reports about their activities."[10] Sharing information with the ICTY about police units in the area and their command structures, as well as the regular reports filed by these units, would help in identifying those responsible for these abuses.

The village of Gornje Obrinje was largely destroyed during the Yugoslav offensive. The village was still smoldering when Human Rights Watch researchers arrived around 11 a.m. on September 29, and sporadic gun fire continued nearby. Most of the homes in the village had been destroyed, and the village bore the marks of a heavy assault. Many of the homes were pockmarked by bullets or shrapnel and some had been hit by tank fire. However, as in many other villages, Human Rights Watch also observed signs of damage inflicted on the village in the aftermath of any fighting. Shot cattle lay strewn around the town, and many free-standing hay stacks and other food supplies had been torched. Some homes appeared to have been set on fire, judging from the fact that they had not sustained any visible bullet or mortar damage.

The Dead at the Delijaj Compound

When Human Rights Watch researchers arrived at the scene of the massacre, local villagers were removing the bodies of the victims from the forest to a burial site in a field called Lluga e Ferizit (in Albanian) near the Delijaj compound. Human Rights Watch observed the bodies of three victims, wrapped in blankets, being carried out from the site on home-made stretchers. One of the bodies was that of an infant, Valmir Delijaj, eighteen months old. Seven other bodies, identified by family members as Zahide, Gentjana, Donjeta, Mehonija, Menduhija, Lumnija, and Hamide, were still lying in the forest, apparently where they had been killed three days before.

Fazli Delijaj - Family Patriarch, Burned to Death

Human Rights Watch encountered a group of international journalists while walking to the forest, who said that they had seen three bodies inside Gornje Obrinje. One body was found inside a home, they said, and had been severely

---

[10]"Serb Police Deny Responsibility for Killings," *Reuters*, September 30, 1998.

burned. According to the evidence available, this was the body of Fazli Delijaj, the ninety-four-year-old patriarch of the Delijaj family. Family members told Human Rights Watch that Fazli Delijaj was an invalid who had remained behind in the village because he was unable to run away to the forest.[11] Jonathan Steele of the *Guardian* (London) described finding the body of Fazli Delijaj in an article about the massacre:

> We walked out of the wood [of the massacre site] to a field where men with spades were starting to dig graves in the damp ground, and on up to the hill to Gornje Obrinje. The first family compound we reached was still smouldering. In a charred living room littered with tiles from the collapsed roof, a villager pointed out the thin torso of a 95-year-old family elder.[12]

Another journalist on the scene, Tom Walker of the *Times* (London), described the condition of Fazli's body in his article:

> A young man crunched through the roof tiles and rubble of a room blackened by heat and flame. In the corner lay a torso, its flesh baked brown. "My father," said the man. Fazli Delijaj, we were told, had been 95.[13]

Bashkim Delijaj, the twenty-one year old son of Fazli Delijaj, discovered the burned body of his father on Monday, September 28. Bashkim had stayed with his father until he was forced to flee shortly before Serbian infantry entered the Delijaj compound. He told Human Rights Watch, "I told my father that I was going to keep the animals out of the cornfields because I didn't want to tell him the truth about the soldiers who were approaching."[14] Bashkim told Human Rights Watch what he found when he returned to the village with his uncle Imer Delijaj two days later:

---

[11]Human Rights Watch interviews, Gornje Obrinje, September 29, 1998.

[12]Jonathan Steele, "Among the 16 victims was a baby, beneath her mother's corpse, and a boy, his throat cut," *Guardian* (London*)*, September 30, 1998.

[13]Tom Walker, "Hidden Horror Betrays the Butchers of Kosovo," *Times (London)*, September 30, 1998.

[14]Human Rights Watch interview with Bashkim Delijaj, Priština, November 11, 1998.

After we found the body of Adem [see below], I told Imer, "Let's go see my father," and we went. I looked through the window, but nothing was left of my father. I saw only the bones, which looked like what we had learned in biology class. He had burned.[15]

Interviewed separately, Imer Delijaj confirmed Bashkim's description of Fazli.[16]

Adem Delijaj

On Monday morning, September 28, Imer Delijaj, a self-acknowledged KLA fighter, and Bashkim Delijaj returned to the Delijaj compound to find out what had happened to their families. Imer told Human Rights Watch how they discovered the body of his brother Adem, thirty-three, near the gate of Imer's home:

When Bashkim and I came to our neighborhood, we saw Ali's and Pajazit's houses burned. Uncle Sherif's house was also burned. When I came to my house, in the entrance I saw Adem, my brother, about four or five meters from the entrance. He was dead, and there were about sixteen bullet casings around his body and near the entrance. He was not mutilated, but he had three bullet wounds to his head and his chest. It was raining and he was my brother, so I could not leave him in the rain, so I dragged him into a covered place and let him rest there. Adem was thirty-three years old, and had never been armed in his life. He never had problems with the government or the KLA.[17]

Bashkim Delijaj, interviewed separately by Human Rights Watch, presented an almost identical version of events.

The last person to see Adem Delijaj alive was fifteen-year-old Blerim Delijaj. Blerim told Human Rights Watch that he was walking toward the house of his uncle, Zeqir Delijaj, together with Zeqir and his other uncle, Adem, at about

---

[15]Human Rights Watch interview with Bashkim Delijaj, Priština, November 11, 1998.

[16]Human Rights Watch interview with Imer Delijaj, Gornje Obrinje, November 10, 1998.

[17]Human Rights Watch interview with Imer Delijaj, Gornje Obrinje, November 10, 1998.

1 p.m. on Saturday, September 26. When they reached Zeqir's home, an armed policeman emerged from the house, ordered the trio to stop, and immediately began shooting at them. Blerim ran towards the Hysenaj compound together with Adem and Zeqir, but soon lost track of the other two men. He told Human Rights Watch, "I was running faster and was the farthest away [from the policeman], so I got away."[18] Zeqir Delijaj was among the persons killed in the forest (see below).

Fourteen Dead in the Forest

Fourteen bodies were found around the forest hide-out of the Delijaj family, in addition to the bodies of four men found around the Delijaj compound itself, bringing the total number of bodies buried on September 29 to eighteen. Several of the bodies in the forest were in the process of being removed for burial when Human Rights Watch researchers arrived at the scene. Local villagers, including Imer Delijaj, who was among the first to find the bodies, reconstructed the location of all persons killed. Human Rights Watch was able to gather photographic and testimonial evidence to establish the identity of all persons found at the massacre site, as well as the conditions in which they were found. The detailed descriptions of the gunshot wounds, knife cuts, and mutilations found on the bodies are disturbing, but are essential to understand that this was not an incidental killing during combat but rather a direct attack on a group of defenseless civilians. All bodies found in the forest were dressed in civilian clothes, and there was no evidence of any resistance to the attack.

The bodies were first discovered by Zenjije Delijaj when she went to the forest on Sunday morning, September 27, at about 8 a.m. to tell Imer's family what had happened to Habib, Hysen and Adem Delijaj (see below). Early Monday morning, Imer and Bashkim Delijaj went to the forest and also saw the fourteen bodies. A U.S. team of the Kosovo Diplomatic Observer Mission (KDOM) visited the site on Monday afternoon. They took extensive photographs and included their findings in that day's confidential report, which has not yet been released to the public.

On Tuesday morning, researchers from Human Rights Watch traveled to the site, as did some international journalists. The victims were buried on Tuesday in the early afternoon while Human Rights Watch researchers were still at the scene.

---

[18]Human Rights Watch interview with Blerim Delijaj, Gornje Obrinje, November 10, 1998.

Ali Delijaj

The body of Ali Delijaj, sixty-eight, was found near the path just as it entered the forest grove. Photographs obtained by Human Rights Watch clearly show that Ali's throat had been slit. The knife that was apparently used in the killing was left lying on his chest; villagers told Human Rights Watch that the knife was his own. Villagers believed that the elderly Ali had remained behind in the village of Gornje Obrinje while the family sought shelter in the forest, and that the police had captured Ali and forced him to lead them to the family's forest shelter before they killed him.

Zejnije Delijaj told Human Rights Watch that, when she found Ali, "there was a scarf covering his face and I saw the blood. I removed the scarf and saw that his throat had been cut."[19] Imer Delijaj told Human Rights Watch how he found Ali's body the next day:

> About thirty meters from the tent, we found the body of Ali Delijaj, sixty-five, who was cut on his throat with his own knife lying on his chest. I turned him and saw he had a wound to the back of the head. I turned him again and placed him back in the same position I had found him. He always had his knife with him for cutting tobacco.[20]

The Delijaj family believes that Ali decided to return to his tobacco storage shed near the Delijaj compound when he was captured by the Serbian police, and was then forced by the police to take them to the forest hideout. According to the family members, Ali had freshly cut tobacco in his pocket when he was killed.

Hava and Pajazit Delijaj

About sixty feet down the forest path from Ali's body was the temporary shelter the Delijaj family had constructed in the forest, a wooden frame with a green tarp covering three foam mattresses. Human Rights Watch saw that the middle mattress was soaked with blood, and that a human brain remained on the mattress on the left side of the shelter. According to diplomatic observers and

---

[19]Human Rights Watch interview with Zejnije Delijaj, Mitrovica, November 11, 1998.

[20]Human Rights Watch interview with Imer Delijaj, Gornje Obrinje, November 10, 1998.

journalists who visited the scene while all of the bodies were still in the forest, the bodies of Hava Delijaj, a sixty-two-year-old woman, and Pajazit Delijaj, a sixty-nine-year-old man, were found in the tent. These sources described Hava Delijaj as having a gunshot wound to the head and a cut throat. The diplomatic sources further observed that Hava's right foot was almost severed from the body, apparently in an attempt to remove the foot with a knife. Pajazit was nearly decapitated with his brain fully removed from the cranium and lying next to his body.

Zejnije Delijaj described to Human Rights Watch what she found inside the tent on September 27:

> I saw Pajazit's body lying on his stomach and part of his head had been blown off. He was on the right side of the tent if you are facing it. The left side of his head was missing, and his brain had slipped between the mattresses. The mattress was filled with blood. Then I saw Hava's body lying outside the tent and her legs were deeply cut with a knife. She was lying on her back and her legs were spread. There was lots of blood around her.[21]

This account was confirmed by Imer and Bashkim Delijaj in separate interviews. Imer told Human Rights Watch that Hava's leg was deeply cut, and that "only a small piece of skin and meat was keeping the leg together."[22] Imer and Bashkim decided to move Hava's body inside the tent, because it was raining.

Down the forest path, a small gully veered off to the right. The bodies of eleven persons, mostly women and children, were found along the narrow gully, which measured only a few hundred feet in length. Most were shot in the head, and the fact that they were found in an area of thick brush supports the conclusion that they were executed at close range, possibly as they attempted to flee from their pursuers.

Hamide, Jeton, Luljeta, and Valmir Delijaj
A group of four bodies was found by family members, diplomatic observers, and journalists a few feet up the narrow gully. This group included one

---

[21]Human Rights Watch interview with Zejnije Delijaj, Mitrovica, November 11, 1998.

[22]Human Rights Watch interview with Imer Delijaj, Gornje Obrinje, November 10, 1998.

of the youngest victims of the attack, eighteen-month-old Valmir Delijaj, found with a blood-splattered face. Jeton Delijaj, a nine-year-old boy, was found close by, reportedly with his throat cut from the jugular to the lower lip by a knife or a bullet.[23]

In his interview with Human Rights Watch, Imer Delijaj described finding these bodies, which included several immediate family members:

> I continued up the gully, and saw my nine-year-old son Jeton. He had a wound from his left ear to his mouth. I hope it was from a bullet and not a knife [so he would not have suffered]. It is the only body which I am not sure how he was killed. One shoe was on and one shoe was off.
>
> Five meters away was my sixty-year-old mother, Hamide, lying on her left side. She had a wound on the right side of her head and a small wound on her chest. I think she was killed with a "warm weapon" [a gun] from a close distance. I think she was shot in the face, not killed with a knife.
>
> Nearby was the body of Luljeta, the pregnant wife of my brother, about to give birth any day. We had even decided on a name for the baby, Malsore, which means "mountain girl" and relates to our suffering in the mountains. Luljeta was the same as Hamide. Their legs were together. She was lying on her right side and she had wounds on the left side of her face. She was hit a little more on the back of the head, and there was a small wound on her nose. A smaller wound was on her left shin.
>
> The other body was that of Valmir, the eighteen-month-old son of Adem. He had a wound on the right side of his face near his jaw, and on his right hand he had a hole but not from a bullet, and other small wounds on his body. His pacifier was hanging on his chest.

---

[23]"Kosovo—Women, Children Massacred," *Reuters*, September 30, 1998; Steele, *Guardian (London)*, September 30, 1998.

I suppose, and I hope, that all the bodies from my mother up were killed with "warm weapons" [guns] from a close range.[24]

The testimony of Zejnije Delijaj, interviewed separately by Human Rights Watch, matched the description of the bodies given by Imer down to specific details. One variation was her description of the pregnant Luljeta. She said:

Luljeta was cut all over, starting from the shoulder going down to the stomach. It was a big cut, like from her breast to her stomach. She was wearing clothes but they were cut too.[25]

Lumnije, Mihane, Menduhije, Diturije and Zeqir Delijaj

Imer found the body of his wife, Lumnije, lying next to his six-week-old daughter Diturije, who amazingly survived the attack. Zejnije had seen the bodies the day before, but had not realized that the baby Diturije was still alive. She told Human Rights Watch:

I saw Lumnije, Imer's wife, lying on her right side and Diturije was under her left arm. Lumnije's face was cut all over, and her left arm above the baby was also cut with a knife. The baby's mouth was full of bood from her mothers' left arm. I did not know that she was still alive.[26]

More than twenty-four hours after Zejnije visited the site, Imer and Bashkim found the young baby alive. Imer recounted the horrible discovery to Human Rights Watch:

I next found the body of my wife, Lumnije. She was lying on her right side, and the two girls were next to her, one in front and one behind. The mother's hand was on the baby [six-week-old Diturije]. At that moment, she opened her eyes, not totally but halfway, and I realized she was alive. I was trying to clean the blood out of her mouth, and she stuck her tongue out a little.

---

[24]Human Rights Watch interview with Imer Delijaj, Gornje Obrinje, November 10, 1998.
    [25]Human Rights Watch interview with Zejnije Delijaj, Mitrovica, November 11, 1998.
    [26]Ibid.

I left the bodies and took the clothes off the baby. It was a terrible smell. I checked her and saw she was not wounded. I dressed her again and covered her in my jacket.[27]

Human Rights Watch visited the baby Diturije on November 8 in Likovac, where she was staying with relatives. Sadly, she died on November 19, reportedly due to a lack of medical care.[28]

Lying nearby were the bodies of four-year-old Menduhije, daughter of Imer and Lumnije, Imer's cousin Zeqir, forty-four, and twenty-five-year-old Mehane, the wife of Adem. Imer described Mihane's condition:

The next body, parallel with another, was Mihane, twenty-five, the mother of Valmir. She was lying on her stomach, and her internal organs were spilling out through a big hole in her back. It looked like an explosion not from a gun but from a grenade.[29]

Photographs obtained by Human Rights Watch confirm the condition of Mihane's body.

Neither Imer not Zejnije got a close look at Menduhije; both only saw that her hair was covered with blood. According to Zejnije, Zeqir was "full of blood from head to toe."[30]

Zahide Delijaj and Her Two Daughters, Donjeta and Gentjana

On top of the thickly wooded gully, Human Rights Watch saw three more bodies. Zahide Delijaj, twenty-seven, was found at the edge of the gully, apparently shot as she was trying to climb out. A bullet had shot away the back of her head. Zahide was only wearing socks, not shoes, suggesting that she may have been resting in the tent at the time of the attack. Her two daughters lay dead immediately behind her. Five-year-old Donjeta had an apparent gunshot wound

---

[27]Human Rights Watch interview with Imer Delijaj, Gornje Obrinje, November 10, 1998.

[28]Julius Strauss, "Massacre Baby Dies For Lack of Care: Medical Aid Too Late To Save Kosovo Survivor," *Daily Telegraph*, November 30, 1998.

[29]Human Rights Watch interview with Imer Delijaj, Gornje Obrinje, November 10, 1998.

[30]Human Rights Watch interview with Zejnije Delijaj, Mitrovica, November 11, 1998.

that had removed part of the right side of her face. Seven-year-old Gentjana had the top of her head removed, apparently by a bullet.

Zejnije became too disturbed before reaching these bodies, and turned back. Imer also gave a limited description of these bodies, partly because he had just found his dead wife and children and was severely traumatized. According to Bashkim, he and Imer briefly went to look at Zahide and her two daughters before returning to Imer's wife and children, where they found Diturije still alive. Imer described what he remembered to Human Rights Watch:

> Donjeta, who was five years old, was lying face down. She had a wound on her left shoulder and behind her right ear... Her face looked deformed, and was turned to the ground.... I can't describe the body of Gentjana, who was seven years old. I cannot remember her wounds so it is better not to talk about it.

> The other body was Zahide Delijaj, their mother. She had a big wound to the top of the head, but her brain was not missing. I did not turn her over because it would be against our traditions.

> After this, I searched for the four missing children,[31] with the baby on my shoulder, but I could not find them.[32]

Both Imer and Bashkim stated that Bashkim was severely traumatized by seeing the bodies of his deceased relatives and was hysterical at times. However, his account of their findings in the forest, given separately to Human Rights Watch, closely mirrors the testimonies given by Imer and Zejnije.

The Killing of Hajriz Delijaj

According to the Council for the Defense of Human Rights and Freedoms, a local human rights group, the body of Hajriz Delijaj, thirty-four, was found in a water well near Gornje Obrinje on October 21, 1998. Hajriz, the husband of massacre victim Zahide Delijaj and father of Gentjana and Donjeta Delijaj, had been missing since the time of the massacre. The Council for the Defense of

---

[31]The children, Besnik (5), Liridona (3), Albert (2), and Arlinda (13 months) were taken by the police to the Hysenaj compound in Gornje Obrinje (see below).

[32]Human Rights Watch interview with Imer Delijaj, Gornje Obrinje, November 10, 1998.

Human Rights and Freedoms reported that, "[t]he victim's corpse was mutilated, his throat was cut and he was shot on his head from close range."[33] Human Rights Watch viewed photos taken during the funeral of Hajriz, and these photos indicate trauma to the head of the victim.

The Killing of Habib, Hysen, Antigona and Mihane Delijaj

In addition to the fourteen members of the Delijaj family hiding in the forest, a smaller group from the family fled from the village and fell victim to a separate series of killings near Gornje Obrinje. This group included Habib and his wife Zejnije; Hysen and his wife Floria; an aunt of Habib named Maliqe; Hysen's two daughters (by an earlier marriage), Antigona and Mihane; and the two young children of Hysen and Floria, named Mentor and Ajete. The story of the survivors of this group, some of the witnesses who were closest to the killings near the Delijaj compound, provide important clues as to what happened during the offensive.

According to separate interviews with Zejnije and Floria, on Friday, September 25, these family members were in Gornje Obrinje when the shelling started around 8 a.m. As the attack started, they fled toward the woods the Albanians call Zabele, where the extended family of Imer Delijaj was sheltering in the makeshift tent. They found all of their relatives alive in the forest and stayed with them during Friday. On Friday night at about 9 p.m., this part of the Delijaj family went back to the Delijaj compound, leaving the extended family of Imer behind in the forest. They hid for the night in a large hole dug by Habib near his home which was covered with leaves.

On Saturday, at about 4 a.m., the family woke and Habib said they should flee into the hills. Habib and his wife, Zejnije, Antigona, Mihane, and Mentor left at this time, leaving Hysen and Floria, Maliqe, and Ajete in the dugout hole. Habib and his family went by foot to Terdevac, where they arrived at about 8 a.m. and started a cooking fire in a field. Almost immediately, shelling started close to the field, and the family was forced to run away. They found shelter in the nearby woods and were told by an acquaintance they encountered that Sherif Delijaj had been wounded and that the Delijaj compound had been burned. As of January 21, 1999, Sherif Delijaj remains missing.

At 5 p.m. on Saturday, Habib decided the group should return to Gornje Obrinje to find out what had happened to Hysen and the others left behind. They

---

[33]Council for the Defense of Human Rights and Freedoms in Pristina, *Report No. 442*, October 18-25, 1998.

walked back to Gornje Obrinje and managed to cross the main road to Likovac despite a large police presence. The group hid as a large convoy of tanks and APCs was leaving Gornje Obrinje and heading back towards Likovac. After waiting half an hour in the bushes, they tried to move but were spotted by the police and came under heavy fire, forcing them to separate. Zejnije Delijaj told Human Rights Watch what happened:

> We tried to approach the compound, but as soon as we stood up we saw infantry, five or six of them, and they immediately started shooting at us. They heard the leaves. We all ran off in different directions. I was crawling along the road away from Likovac. Antigona is all I saw as she lay on the ground hiding from the bullets. I was the closest to the police, and I could feel the dirt flying against my leg as the bullets hit the ground.
>
> I didn't know which direction I was crawling. They were constantly shooting. They thought we were KLA. First they were shooting with machine guns but then they started using other weapons. All the time I was crawling I could hear the shooting until 1 a.m. I didn't know where the others were.[34]

Throughout the night, Zejnije, now separated from the rest of her family, was fired upon by the police when she tried to move. While crawling, she fell into a deep hole, injuring her face and losing consciousness for several hours (her injuries were still visible when she was interviewed by Human Rights Watch more than a month later). On Sunday morning, she reached the Hysenaj compound and was again forced to seek shelter when police fired at her from the direction of Likovac. Later, she said, she was briefly detained by a group of police in dark-brown or grey camouflage uniforms with helmets, possibly members of the anti-terrorist police (SAJ). She was allowed to leave and managed to return to the Delijaj compound which was completely burned down by the time she arrived. When she passed the house of Imer Delijaj, she found Adem Delijaj's body near the gate (see above).

Zejnije then went to the hiding place that Habib had dug to see if anyone was there. She found only the elderly Maliqe, who told her that Habib had returned

---

[34]Human Rights Watch interview with Zejnije Delijaj, Mitrovica, November 11, 1998.

during the night and told everyone that they had been shot at and that he was convinced that Zejnije, Mihane and Antigona had been killed. According to Zejnije, Maliqe also told her that Habib had taken Floria, Hysen, Mentor, and Ajete to go find out what had happened to Zejnije and his two daughters. At 7:30 a.m., Floria returned to the hiding place with Mentor and Ajete and said that Habib and Hysen had been killed by the police during the search.

Zejnije said Floria explained to her how Habib and Hysen had been killed. The group had walked toward the police while looking for Zejnije, Mihane, and Antigona. The police stopped them and interrogated them about the location of the KLA. Habib reportedly replied that he had come only to retrieve the bodies of his wife and the daughters of his brother Hysen. The police then asked about the whereabouts of Habib's son Dr. Sami Delijaj—doctors have repeatedly been targeted by police, who believe they are providing medical care to the KLA[35]—and Habib replied that he was in Priština. Floria then told Zejnije that the police began to beat Habib. When Habib fell down, a policeman loaded his rifle and fired at Habib, killing him. Hysen, who had mental problems according to family members, started waving his arms and screaming loudly when he saw his brother killed. He himself was then shot twice in the head. Floria told Zejnije that Mentor was screaming and ran toward Habib, but a policeman slapped the young boy and said either "Brže," which means "faster" in Serbian, or "Beži," which means "get out of here."

Journalists who visited the scene on September 29, 1998, described finding the bodies of Habib Delijaj, fifty-five, and Hysen Delijaj, fifty-two, at the end of a set of tank tracks. According to one report, the top of Hysen Delijaj's head had been shot off.[36] The location of the bodies according to journalists is consistent with the account Floria gave to Zejnije.

Imer Delijaj also described finding Habib's and Hysen's bodies. He said:

> According to what Floria said, I looked for the bodies on Monday, September 28, and Tuesday. Around 7:00 or 7:30 a.m. I found them.... Habib was mutilated in a terrible way. His brain was out. He was cut with a knife on his back. He had

---

[35]See a preliminary report by Physicians for Human Rights, "Medical group documents systematic and pervasive abuses by Serbs against Albanian Kosovar health professionals and Albanian Kosovar patients," December 23, 1998.

[36]Jonathan Steele, *Guardian*, September 30, 1998.

bruises on his face, but no wounds on his chest. He had a cross
cut on his back and stab wounds around the lower torso.[37]

Human Rights Watch also conducted a separate interview with Floria.
Her account is largely consistent with Zejnije's and Imer's but does contain some
minor discrepancies. According to family members, including Dr. Sami Delijaj,
Floria has a history of mental problems as a result of having had meningitis as a
child. The main difference is over the precise location of Habib's and Hysen's
death: according to Floria's direct testimony, the group was at Floria's home
collecting some goods when the police detained and killed the two men, rather than
on the road where the bodies were found.

Many other details of Floria's account, however, are consistent with what
Zejnije says Floria told her on September 27. In both accounts, Habib asked the
police about his daughters and was questioned by the police about the KLA for a
very short time. Both accounts describe how Habib was beaten and killed first, and
how Hysen was killed after he became hysterical about Habib's death. Small details
are consistent throughout, such as the fact that the policeman loaded his rifle after
Habib was beaten and that Mentor tried to run to his uncle but was sent away by
a policeman. Looking at the physical evidence at the scene, Human Rights Watch
believes that the first account Floria gave to Zenjija is the most probable version
of events. Regardless, both accounts and the physical evidence lead to the same
conclusion: Habib and Hysen Delijaj were summarily murdered by Serbian police.

Another detail consistent in Floria's and Zejnije's accounts is the presence
in Gornje Obrinje of an ethnic Albanian policeman named Xhafer Qorri.
According to Floria's direct testimony, and the testimony of Zejnije, Habib
recognized Qorri while they were being questioned by the police. Floria did not
know Qorri herself, but heard Habib mention his name. According to Floria, Qorri
left the scene before Habib and Hysen were killed, but it is certain that Qorri would
have been able to identify the policemen who killed Habib and Hysen, as well as
some of the others involved in the Gornje Obrinje action. But his testimony will
never be heard.

Xhafer Qorri was shot and killed together with two local Serbs at the
municipal power station in Glogovac on December 11, 1998. Human Rights
Watch learned that Qorri had been responsible for policing five villages in the
Glogovac area since 1968, including Donje and Gornje Obrinje. He had recently

---

[37]Human Rights Watch interview with Imer Delijaj, Gornje Obrinje, November
10, 1998.

The body of Ali Koludra, sixty-two. An eyewitness described to Human Rights Watch how Serbian policemen executed Ali by crushing his skull with an axe. Gornje Obrinje, September 29, 1998. © 1999 Human Rights Watch.

come out of retirement and lived in Glogovac with his family. This was not the first time he had been attacked, since Albanians in the area knew that he worked for the police.

While at the scene of the massacre on September 29, Human Rights Watch was told by surviving Delijaj family members that the two young girls, Antigona and Mihane Delijaj, fourteen and sixteen respectively, were missing. As discussed above, the two girls went missing after being shot at near the road to Likovac on the evening of Saturday, September 26.

The decomposing bodies of the two girls were found about one kilometer from the Delijaj compound on October 4, 1998, by members of the Delijaj family. Human Rights Watch visited the site where the bodies were found, just off the main road leading from Gornje Obrinje to Likovac. A few meters from the site was a small, recently dug hole reinforced with stones, which Imer Delijaj claimed was a bunker dug by the Serbian police, who were guarding the road. Human Rights Watch inspected the bunker and found an empty amunition box for 7.62 mm bullets issued to the Yugoslav forces. Allegations by the family and the Council for the Defense of Human Rights and Freedoms[38] that the two girls had been raped before being murdered could not be confirmed by Human Rights Watch.

The Killings at the Hysenaj Compound of Gornje Obrinje

Of the members of the Delijaj family who were present at the make-shift shelter in the forest, only four young children survived: five-year-old Besnik, three-year-old Liridona, thirteen-month-old Arlinda, and two-year-old Albert. Human Rights Watch met five-year-old Besnik, but did not attempt to interview him because of his age and the traumatic nature of the events he may have witnessed. A psychologist who was treating Besnik, Dr. Gani Halilaj, told Human Rights Watch that the young boy was suffering from classic symptoms of post-traumatic stress syndrome; namely, being uncommunicative and frequently staring off into space, a stark contrast with his bright and talkative personality prior to the incident in the forest.[39]

An uncle of Besnik told Human Rights Watch that Besnik had not given an overall account of the massacre, but he had told family members bits of information which strongly suggested that he had witnessed at least some of the

---

[38]See "CDHRF: "Two new victims of the massacre of the Delijaj family found," *ARTA*, October 5, 1998.

[39]Human Rights Watch interview with Dr. Gani Halilaaj, Banjice, November 12, 1998.

forest massacre. According to the uncle, Besnik told him that he knows how to load a gun because he saw the police do it, and he described policemen in camouflage paint being present in the forest.[40] According to the Belgrade-based Humanitarian Law Center (HLC), a respected local human rights group, Besnik also described to his uncle Imer how he saw Ali Delijaj killed with a blow to the head by a "black man"—perhaps a policeman with camouflage paint on his face or wearing a ski mask.[41]

How and why Besnik and the three other children survived remains unclear. For whatever reason, at least one policeman took the children and brought them unharmed to the Hysenaj compound in Gornje Obrinje about two kilometers from the massacre site. Human Rights Watch first saw the four children on September 29, just before visiting the massacre site near the Delijaj compound. At that time, an elderly women, Shehide Hysenaj, showed Human Rights Watch researchers the bodies of three people killed by the police, including her elderly husband Rrustem (see below). The four children were also present and Shehide told Human Rights Watch that, "these children saved my life." A second visit to Shehide by Human Rights Watch in November revealed how the three victims were killed, and how the four children apparently survived.[42]

According to Shehide, by the time the police reached the Hysenaj compound of Gornje Obrinje on September 27, most of the villagers had fled with their possessions into the nearby forest, called, in Albanian, Brija e Terdefcit. Aside from Shehide, three villagers remained in the compound: Shedide's husband Rrustem, seventy-three, and a displaced couple from Gremnik village, Ali Koludra, sixty-two, and his wife Hyra Koludra, fifty. The four were having dinner on Saturday, September 27, when policemen entered the compound and started burning homes. Shehide described to Human Rights Watch how she lost contact with the other three people that Saturday night. She told Human Rights Watch:

> When we were sitting in the yard, the police started burning in
> the village, and they started burning our house. Ali, Hyra, and
> Rrustem ran toward the house to see what was happening. I
> remained in the yard near our well and spent all night alone. I

---

[40]Human Rights Watch interview with uncle of Besnik Delijaj, Drenica, November 12, 1998.

[41]Humanitarian Law Center, *Mass Killings at Gornje Obrinje Village, 26-27 September 1998* (November 1998).

[42]Human Rights Watch interview with Shehide Hysenaj, Trstenik, November 12, 1998.

> couldn't see them anymore. The chickens were escaping from
> the flames and coming toward the place I was sitting.[43]

Early Sunday morning, Shehide went to the forest in an unsuccessful attempt to locate the members of the Hysenaj family hiding there. At about 7 or 8 a.m., she decided to return to her burned home to find the three people she had left. When she reached the well where she had been sheltering, she noticed a group of about ten policemen who ordered her to come near in Serbian. When she approached, she noticed several other groups of policemen milling about, as well as many army tanks on the road bisecting the town. The policemen grabbed her, raised her dress to check for weapons, and took her to the home of Shaban Nasufi, the only home in the village left unburned. Inside the home, she found Ali and Hyra, as well as four young children—the survivors of the forest massacre:

> When I was inside, I saw Ali and Hyra alive. They were sitting
> in a kind of line. They brought me the four children, and
> ordered me to feed them and send them to bed. Besnik had
> blood on his neck and sweater. In the meantime, the police were
> interrogating Ali and Hyra in Serbian.[44]

Shehide described to Human Rights Watch how the police questioned the three persons about their ties to the KLA. As Shehide did not speak Serbian, Ali and a policeman who spoke Albanian translated for her during the interogation. The police questioned the three about who belonged to the KLA, and accused the two women of providing food to KLA members and knowing where the KLA was hiding. She then described to Human Rights Watch how she witnessed Hyra being murdered by the police:

> They demanded money from us, from Hyra as well. The police
> accused Hyra of giving food to the KLA. They then slapped
> Hyra, and two of the police grabbed her by the arms and took
> her out of the house. They killed her immediately, and mutilated
> her arms by cutting them with a knife or an axe, I am not sure

---

[43]Ibid.
[44]Ibid.

which. Both the children and I witnessed the killing, I was
almost going crazy and the children were screaming.[45]

After killing Hyra, the police continued to interrogate Ali in front of
Shehide. According to Shehide, the police subjected Ali to a severe beating,
punching him in the face and kicking him in the ribs with their boots. The police
also continued to interrogate Shehide, asking her where her two sons were and
again accusing her of providing food to the KLA. An Albanian-speaking
policeman wearing an all-black uniform, in contrast to the other policemen who
were wearing blue and black camouflage uniforms, led the interrogation. Shehide
described the Albanian-speaking policeman as sturdy and big, with a machine gun,
a knife, and a radio. While they were being interrogated, the police continued
purposefully to burn homes in the village.
        At about 2 p.m., according to Shehide, a new group of policemen entered
the home, and brutally killed Ali. She said:

> At about 2 p.m., another group of policemen came, and they
> were behaving very brutally, they were merciless. They asked
> Ali a question, and as he was answering they took him out and
> killed him. I went out together with the children, screaming and
> crying for Ali. We saw Ali killed. Two Serb police were
> carrying him by his armpits. A third policeman took the axe
> used for cutting wood and hit Ali with the axe on top of the
> head. The brain came out. Afterwards, they were hitting him in
> the sides with the axe. They were merciless. After that, they left
> all together in a group.[46]

Shehide remained in the house, peering out of a window and observing the
police leaving, but was too afraid to leave the house with the screaming children.
When she reassured herself that the police had left, she went to the yard of her
house and found the body of her husband Rrustem in the yard:

> I took the children and went to the yard of my house. I wanted
> to tell my neighbor about the killings. Suddenly, I spotted my

---

[45]Ibid.
[46]Ibid.

The mother of Driton Hysenaj at the funeral of her murdered son. Gornje Obrinje, November 14, 1998. © Human Rights Watch.

husband, Rrustem. Rrustem was also killed, probably with an axe to his head. His chest also had slashes.[47]

The detailed testimony of Shehide is corroborated by significant physical evidence. Other witnesses interviewed by Human Rights Watch at the funeral of Driton Hysenaj confirmed that they had seen Shehide together with the four Delijaj children, Ali, and Hyra in police custody.[48] Human Rights Watch researchers at the Hysenaj compound on September 29 observed and photographed the bodies of Rrustem Halilaj and Ali and Hyra Kaludra prior to their burial. Their injuries were consistent with Shehide's account. In addition, Shehide's brief testimony of September 29 was consistent with the more substantial statement she gave to Human Rights Watch on November 12. Imer Delijaj and many other members of the Hysenaj and Delijaj families, interviewed separately, confirmed that the four children who survived the massacre had been brought by the police to the Hysenaj compound.

The Murder of Driton Hysenaj
Because of the heavy fighting in the Gornje Obrinje area, the approximately 150 residents of the Hysenaj compound fled with their possesions into the forest on Friday, September 25, leaving only a few elderly members of the extended family behind. The Hysenaj clan set up camp in the forest at a place called, in Albanian, Brija e Terdefcit, less than a kilometer away from their compound, and remained there for the next two days. According to the witnesses interviewed by Human Rights Watch at the funeral of Driton, most of the persons staying in the forest were women, children, and the elderly, with only a few younger men. None of them were armed, according to those present.

On Sunday, September 27, some time between 11 a.m. and 3 p.m., Serb forces surrounded the displaced community in the forest, apparently after following a young boy to the forest camp. Daut Hysenaj, who was present in the forest, told Human Rights Watch what happened next:

---

[47]Ibid.
[48]Human Rights Watch interviews, Gornje Obrinje, November 14, 1998.

The police separated the men from the women, and then stripped
the men naked at that very place. Then they bound the men two
by two and ordered us to walk to the Hysenaj compound.[49]

The stripsearch conducted by the police turned up no weapons, "not even
a jack knife," according to Brahim Hysenaj, who was also present.[50] While being
searched, the men were subjected to a severe beating, and were hit with rifle butts.
The jaw of one man, Raif Hysenaj, was broken at this time.[51]

The police selected a group of twenty-two men, allowed them to dress,
and marched them back to the Hysenaj compound, where they were ordered to sit
in front of a hedge. According to Brahim Hysenaj, who was one of the twenty-two
men, there were several hundred policemen in the Hysenaj compound by the time
the men arrived. The men witnessed the police burning the homes around them.
Brahim told Human Rights Watch:

We saw the police burning the houses. They used some type of
spray with a pump to spray the area of the house, and when they
shoot, the spray ignites immediately. I saw them spraying the
houses, but we didn't dare to look any more.[52]

The police continued to beat the men at the compound. Daut Hysenaj told Human
Rights Watch:

The policemen started beating us again. As we were lined in a
queue, they came to us. The first group of policemen slapped us,
and the second group started punching us. A third group began
hitting us with their rifle butts. They asked no questions. This
lasted about fifteen or thirty minutes. We were handcuffed or
tied while being beaten.[53]

---

[49]Human Rights Watch interview with Daut Hysenaj, Trstenik, November 12,
1998.

[50]Human Rights Watch interview with Brahim Hysenaj, Glogovac, November 12,
1998.

[51]Ibid.

[52]Ibid.

[53]Human Rights Watch interview with Basram Hysenaj, Glogovac, November 12,
1998.

After the beating, the policemen appropriated a tractor, burning all the food loaded in its attached lorry. The policemen ordered the twenty-two men, still tied two by two, to climb into the lorry, and they were driven on the dirt road to Likovac, the functional headquarters for the government's offensive. Both Daut and Brahim Hysenaj, interviewed separately, described a nightmarish journey that included the murder by knife of one young boy, Driton Hysenaj. Brahim Hysenaj said:

> While being taken to Likovac, we had to pass through the Delijaj compound, and we saw the policemen burning the houses all along the road. The driver of the tractor would stop by the road and let the policemen beat us. They beat us with whatever was available, including wooden sticks.[54]

When the men finally arrived in Likovac, some of the policemen shouted that the tractor was carrying captured KLA members. Without warning, according to Daut and Brahim, an unidentified policeman ran up to the trailer, grabbed sixteen-year-old Driton Hysenaj by the hair, and slit his throat with a large knife. Brahim said:

> In Likovac, the police claimed that they had brought in some KLA, so in one moment, a policeman ran up to the tractor, grabbed this guy by the hair [Driton Hysenaj] and slit his throat. I was wearing white socks and they became red because the tractor did not have a place to let the blood drain. Another policeman cut the rope of the guy tied to Driton with a foot-long knife. The other guy tied to Driton [Qerim Hysenaj] was very afraid and tried to move far from the police because he thought they might kill him as well. His arm was already broken from the previous beatings.[55]

According to Brahim, himself a former Yugoslav army officer, the policeman who killed Driton was wearing a brown, black, and yellow camouflage uniform and a darker handkerchief on his head. The witness specifically distinguished the killer's uniform from the blue and black camouflage uniforms

---

[54]Human Rights Watch interview with Brahim Hysenaj, Glogovac, November 12, 1998.

[55]Ibid.

worn by many of the regular MUP forces.[56] According to sources familiar with
MUP uniforms, the brown, black, and yellow uniforms are worn by the special
anti-terrorist force, or SAJ (Specijalna Antiteroristicka Jedinica). The eyewitness
also claimed that many other policemen in the area witnessed the killing of Driton,
and that none of the policemen attempted to intervene.[57]

        The body of Driton Hysenaj was taken away by the police, and remained
unaccounted for until November 13, 1998, when his remains were found in a
shallow grave in Likovac by a local villager gathering soil to rebuild his home. A
Human Rights Watch researcher attended Driton's burial in Gornje Obrinje on
November 14, and observed that the severely decomposed remains were dressed
in civilian clothing. The advanced state of decomposition made it impossible to
document the alleged knife wound without a forensic investigation.

Arbitrary Detention and Abuses in Custody

        The ordeal of the twenty-two men taken from the Hysenaj compound to
Likovac did not end with the murder of Driton Hysenaj. After the murder, the
remaining twenty-one men were told to get out of the tractor and were surrounded
by a crowd of policemen which was estimated by one of the men to have been as
many as 500. The Yugoslav forces in Likovac at the time included regular MUP
paramilitary police, special anti-terrorist units (SAJ), and Yugoslav Army troops,
as observed by the surviving men. The men were again beaten by some of these
forces with wooden clubs and metal pipes until a police commander intervened and
stopped the beatings. The men were then forced to board an army truck, which took
them to the Glogovac police station. On the way to the police station, the army
truck, driven by soldiers, stopped at the Rezalla and Morina police checkpoints and
allowed the policemen on duty to beat the men some more.[58]

        At Glogovac police station, the men joined several hundred others who
had been detained during the recent offensive. Witnesses told Human Rights
Watch that they were extensively interrogated by the police about their ties to the
KLA. One detainee claimed that one of the policemen who interrogated them in
Glogovac was Xhafer Qorri, the ethnic Albanian policeman who other witnesses
claimed was present around Gornje Obrinje during the offensive. According to

---

        [56]Ibid.
        [57]According to Brahim, the commanding officer was in an army uniform and
appeared to be of middle rank. About 400 policemen were in Likovac, he said, wearing a
variety of uniforms, including ordinary policemen from the MUP and SAJ forces.
        [58]Human Rights Watch interview with Brahim Hysenaj, Glogovac, November 12,
1998.

Brahim Hysenaj, when one of the detainees told Qorri about the death of Driton Hysenaj, Qorri handed the detainee over to another policemen who threatened to go to the house of the detainee and rape his wife and daughters.[59] While the men were being interrogated and beaten, the police turned on the engine of an armored personnel carrier to drown out the screaming. One witness described being beaten with wooden clubs during his interrogation.

The detainees were forced to sing Serbian songs by the police. According to Brahim Hysenaj, his brother was fed up with the Serb provocations and stood up during the singing to say "Hail Kosova Republic." His brother was beaten unconscious by several policemen, Brahim said, and the others were warned that they would all be killed if a similar incident happened again. Another man, Faik Asllani, was brutally beaten in front of the men, ostensibly because some members of the Asllani clan are major figures in the KLA. According to Brahim Hysenaj, "It was raining and they just beat him and threw him in the gutter and left him. We just saw his chest moving and realized he was still breathing and alive."

Most of the men were released beginning Wednesday, September 30, 1998, but Brahim Hysenaj claimed to Human Rights Watch that fifty-six men were taken to Priština and charged with terrorism. One elderly man, sixty-year-old Zymer Hysenaj, was released on Wednesday and was so exhausted that he had to be helped home. He was left at a place near his home by his fellow detainees, but has not been seen since.

Hundreds of other men were arrested during the offensive in the Drenica region and the Čičavica mountains, and some were held at Glogovac police station simultaneously with and prior to the arrival of the men from the Hysenaj compound. One other group of men included Avni Hysenaj, the twenty-five-year-old son of Shehide and Rrustem Hysenaj (see above), who was among those rounded up by the police in the Čičavica mountains. Avni Hysenaj told Human Rights Watch that he had been with a large group of internally displaced persons, hiding in the forest near a place called, in Albanian, Fusha e Korhices, when they were surrounded by a combined force of police and military (including tanks) on Wednesday, September 24, 1998. The police allowed the displaced persons to return to a nearby village, and ordered them to bring all their possessions and tractors out of the forest, threatening to destroy anything left behind. At 5 a.m. on Thursday, September 25, the police surrounded the village and began to separate the men from the women. About 200 men were videotaped, photographed, and their personal details processed by the police. According to Avni Hysenaj, the

---

[59]Ibid.

police commander at the scene identified himself as the commander of the police station at Srbica.[60] A few older men were then released, while the other men were taken to the yard of a house where policemen were cooking food and some soldiers were milling around. Avni Hysenaj told Human Rights Watch about the beatings that ensued:

> We were sent to a house yard where the police were cooking. They ordered us to put our hands on the cars and they started kicking us. They took our wallets and money. Then, they ordered us to put our hands against the wall and we were kept there for one and a half hours, until a truck to transport us came.
>
> Three youngsters from Prekaz were taken into the house and brutally beaten. We had to wait until this beating was finished. I saw them when they came out, they were bleeding with broken bones in their faces. The police said they were cousins of Adem Jashari[61] and other such things.[62]

When the wives of the men attempted to intervene and begged the police for their husbands' release, the police responded with profanities and threats that all of the men would be killed. The men were then forced to walk down a road with burning hedges on both sides toward the truck, where the police again beat them in order to force the estimated 200 men into a single truck. The men were taken to Glogovac, where they were again beaten with clubs, metal pipes, and boots while unloading from the truck, according to Avni Hysenaj.

The large group of men from many areas of the Drenica region was kept at the Glogovac police station in a large concrete room until they gradually began to be released on Saturday, September 27. The men were fingerprinted, tested for traces of gunpowder, and they were interrogated aggressively about their ties to the

---

[60]Human Rights Watch interview with Avni Hysenaj,Trstenik, November 12, 1998.

[61]Adem Jashari was the main figure of the Jashari clan from Donji Prekaz and a local member of the KLA. Special police forces attacked the Jashari family's compound on March 5, 1998, killing an estimated fifty-eight people, including eighteen women and ten children under the age of sixteen. (See Human Rights Watch report: "Humanitarian Law Violations in Kosovo," pp. 26-32).

[62]Human Rights Watch interview with Avni Hysenaj,Trstenik, November 12, 1998.

KLA and the whereabouts of missing Serbs. Avni Hysenaj told Human Rights Watch:

> First, they fingerprinted us three times each, and then they conducted gunpowder tests on our faces and hands. They were asking who belonged to the KLA. They told me that I had been a [KLA] soldier and a guard, and I told them that it was not so... A fat policeman, speaking Serbian, asked me who had killed Bulatović from Likovac. I told them I didn't know, that it was not my interest as an ordinary man...
>
> Then another policeman entered and told me, "Yes, now you will tell for sure who killed Bulatović." They ordered me to put my hands out and hit me with a club ten times on each hand. After this, I could no longer hold out my hands so they held them for me and continued the beating. Then they forced me to bend over a table, and two policemen beat me on the lower back, buttocks, and thighs. They asked me again who had abducted Bulatović, and I replied: "I do not know, comrade." The policeman said he was not my comrade because I was KLA and he was a policeman. I told him that if we could not be comrades, let it be okay. They then beat me again for those words. The one policeman kicked me on the chest with his boots. I told the policeman he was torturing me for no reason, as I was innocent. He replied, "This is nothing."[63]

By coincidence, Human Rights Watch briefly encountered Avni Hysenaj on September 30, 1998, two days after his release from Glogovac police station, while documenting the deaths at the Hysenaj compound. At that time, he showed Human Rights Watch researchers the deep bruises on his lower back and buttocks that were sustained, he claimed, from the beatings in the Glogovac police station. The injuries, long, thin bruises on his lower back and buttocks, photographed by Human Rights Watch, were consistent with his account, at that time and later, of the beatings he had endured.

---

[63]Human Rights Watch interview with Avni Hysenaj, Trstenik, November 12, 1998.

Many other serious beatings and abuses took place at the Glogovac police station during the three-day period the men were detained. One of the detainees claimed to Human Rights Watch that he saw a military truck being loaded with refrigerators, televisions, VCRs and other electronics that had been stored at the Glogovac police station, and were probably looted from ethnic Albanian homes. On several occasions, Human Rights Watch researchers traveling in Kosovo personally observed policemen in uniform removing private property from abandoned ethnic Albanian homes. On one occasion, the police took a young man from Krajkova outside the holding room, injured him in the leg, and then told the men: "Look what the KLA has done, they have wounded this man. Do not join the KLA, because they will wound you." According to a witness, the police then took the wounded man away, possibly to the Ferrous Nickel plant,[64] and they never saw the wounded man again.

On another occasion, a particularly abusive police officer of Montenegrin origin who said he belonged to Vojislav Šešelj's Radical Party ordered all the detainees to kneel with their heads to the ground. After an estimated two hours, a panic ensued when a group of policemen approached the group and unsheathed their knives. Avni Hysenaj told Human Rights Watch what happened next:

> The police took the person who shouted the alarm, and took him into the police station to beat him. Then they handcuffed him to the raised barrel of a tank, and each policeman came in turn to beat him in front of us. He was getting tired and started slumping, and we could see the handcuff cutting into the flesh and the blood running down his arm.[65]

After this beating, another detainee tried to escape after asking to use the toilet. When he was recaptured, the police put him in a doghouse and forced him to bark like a dog, Avni Hysenaj told Human Rights Watch. The policemen also forced the detainees to sing Serbian nationalist songs, such as:

Ko to laze?	Who is lying?
Ko to kaze:	Who is saying:

---

[64]There are credible but unproven reports that the Ferrous Nickel plant in Glogovac was used by the police as a temporary detention facility.

[65]Human Rights Watch interview with Avni Hysenaj, Trstenik, November 12, 1998.

Srbija je mala?	Serbia is small?
Nije mala!	It is not small!
Nije mala!	It is not small!
Tri put' ratovala!	It fought in three wars!
Dvanajste je,	Nineteen twelve,
Dvanajste je	Nineteen twelve
Turcin udario!	The Turks attacked!
Trinajste je,	Nineteen thirteen,
Trinajste je	Nineteen thirteen
Srbin pobedio!	The Serbs won!
Cetrnajste,	Nineteen fourteen,
Cetrnajste	Nineteen fourteen
Svaba udario!	The Krauts attacked!
Osamnajste,	Nineteen eighteen,
Osamnajste	Nineteen eighteen
Srbin pobedio!	The Serbs won!
Cet'rest prve,	Forty-one,
Cet'rest prve	Forty-one
Svaba udario!	The Krauts attacked!
Cet'rest pete,	Forty-five,
Cet'rest pete	Forty-five
Srbin pobedio!	The Serbs won!

According to Avni Hysenaj, Glogovac police commander Porišić was present during most of the beatings, and only intervened once to stop the beatings towards the end of the ordeal.

The tests for gunpowder came back negative for most of this group of detainees. Most of these detainees began to be released in groups on Saturday, September 26. According to the detainees, at least seven persons tested positive for gunpowder, were sent to Priština, and have not been heard from since.

IV. MASSACRE OF THIRTEEN MEN AT GOLUBOVAC

On Saturday, September 26, 1998, the same day as the forest massacre in Gornje Obrinje, Yugoslav forces summarily killed thirteen men who were detained at a compound in the village of Golubovac.[66] Human Rights Watch visited the scene of the execution on September 29, shortly after the bodies of the thirteen men had been claimed by their family for burial, and conducted interviews at that time, as well as on two additional visits to the village on October 1 and November 9, 1998. The following is an account of the events surrounding the Golubovac killings, based on the testimonies of the witnesses interviewed by Human Rights Watch and the physical evidence found at the scene.

According to Adem Hoxhaj, the entire village of Golubovac decided to evacuate to the forest when shelling began in the early morning of September 25 from Cerovik and Pločica. At about 9 a.m., several thousand civilians, mostly women and children and the elderly from Golubovac and neighboring villages, as well as internally displaced persons staying with relatives in the area, fled to a place in the forest about three kilometers away from Golubovac called Livadhe e Shalës (in Albanian). The villagers took their tractors and some possessions with them and built plastic shelters in the forest. In the early afternoon, Adem Hoxhaj and some other villagers returned to the village to open the doors of their homes, in the belief that the Yugoslav forces would then not burn the homes. At about 3 p.m., Adem saw tanks and APCs entering the village and fled back into the forest.[67]

Adem's brother, fifty-five-year-old Musli Hoxhaj, told Human Rights Watch how the villagers spent Friday night:

> All night Friday, we stayed in the forest. It was raining, and there was shelling from Pločica and Mlečane. We were in the valley, and the police were shooting from one side of the valley to the other ridge, right over our heads.[68]

---

[66]Like many villages in the area, the village of Golubovac is divided into several distinct parts and compounds. The events described in this section took place in the "old" part of Golubovac.

[67]Human Rights Watch interview with Adem Hoxhaj, Golubovac, November 9, 1998.

[68]Human Rights Watch interview with Musli Hoxhaj, Golubovac, November 9, 1998.

On Saturday morning, the villagers started some cooking fires in the forest, and quickly found themselves surrounded by Serb police. Adem Hoxhaj had gone out early in the morning and had encountered a police commander, but managed to escape back to the camp to tell the civilians that they were surrounded by police. He described the police commander to Human Rights Watch:

> The commander had a black bandana covering his hair, which made it difficult to recognize him. He was wearing a normal blue camouflage uniform. He was tall, about two meters, and was fat and muscular. He had a pale white face painted with black and green camouflage paint.[69]

When Adem returned to the camp and informed his fellow villagers that they were surrounded, many began to cry. It was decided that Adem and some other elders would go back out of the forest to meet the police. When they met the same police commander, he instructed the elders to return to the forest and to order everyone into a field in the nearby valley. According to Selman Morina, the sole survivor of the extrajudicial execution that followed, the police told the civilians that they would be safe. He said:

> At about 8 or 9 a.m. on Saturday, the Serbs came into the forest. They told us that everyone in the forest must come out into a field where they could see us, and that we would be safe. They sent some old men to convey this message.[70]

Adem Hoxhaj, who speaks limited Serbian, was chosen by the police commander as an informal interpreter. He described what happened next:

> I asked the people to get out of the tents and into the valley, and this is what everybody did. The police told us to stand in a group and line up. The police commander then told me to tell all men older than eighteen to come out and separate from the group. He then changed his mind, and asked for all the men

---

[69]Human Rights Watch interview with Adem Hoxhaj, Golubovac, November 9, 1998.

[70]Human Rights Watch interview with Selman Morina, Golubovac, October 1, 1998.

older than sixteen to come out. ... After about twenty minutes, I
was asked to tell the group that all women, children, and older
people could go home.[71]

While the civilians were heading home, the police thoroughly searched the
tractors and tents in the forest. According to witnesses, the police took any
valuable possessions they found, including gold. Adem Hoxhaj told Human Rights
Watch that he lost the gold jewelry of six women (a traditional form of family
wealth) from his family and was almost killed when he protested. Musli Hoxhaj
also reported losing 3,000 DM to the police when he was in the valley. After
searching the displaced persons' camp, the police proceeded to burn the tractors by
igniting the mattresses and straw they carried. Only a single clip of bullets was
recovered from the large camp, according to those present, suggesting that there
was no large KLA presence in the forest. Selman Morina, one of the group of men
who remained behind, told Human Rights Watch how the police began to process
the men left in the forest:

> After they sent the women and children away, the police began
> to check the men for weapons and other signs that they belonged
> to the KLA. They then sent us to follow the women and
> children, but we were still kept separate. One policeman came
> and divided us, men from men. He pointed out the men he
> wanted to come out of the crowd, and chose about twenty or
> twenty-five of us. He took us to a separate place. The police
> further divided our group by age. My brother and I were in the
> group, and the older ones were separated and allowed to leave.
>
> They then began to question us, asking where our weapons were.
> They were beating us. Ten or fifteen police questioned us, and
> they repeatedly changed the policemen asking questions. We
> were still in the field at this time. We had to put our hands
> behind our head, and were questioned in the group, not
> individually. They were kicking us with their boots and hitting

---

[71]Human Rights Watch interview with Adem Hoxhaj, Golubovac, November 9,
1998.

us with weapons. I was hit on the head, on my legs, and on my back.[72]

When they returned to Golubovac, the villagers found a large police and military presence, with armored personnel carriers and tanks parked throughout the village. Most of the villagers were allowed to return home, but police had set up a temporary command center at the compound of Adem Hoxhaj and did not allow anyone to enter the area. Several hundred civilians, including Adem's family, instead sought shelter at the adjacent compound of his brother, Musli Hoxhaj, where they remained until after the police had left the village.

A Sole Survivor
Miraculously, one of the group of fourteen men whom the police tried to execute managed to survive. Human Rights Watch located and interviewed Selman Morina on October 1, and then passed the information along to the relevant international agencies who could help guarantee the safety of this crucial witness. A few days later, Morina and his family were escorted out of the country to safety.

Morina's detailed testimony to Human Rights Watch of the events surrounding the execution is consistent with the evidence of other witnesses, and with the physical evidence found by Human Rights Watch at the scene of the execution. Selman Morina told Human Rights Watch:

> They brought us to the garden where the execution took place. Until the execution, our hands had to remain behind our heads. We reached the garden about two hours after we were first gathered in the field. We were then kept about two hours with our hands behind our heads on the road in front of the garden. The last time I saw the women and children was in the field, so I do not know where they were taken. We were made to kneel with our hands behind our heads and faces touching the ground. We were not beaten when we were in the road next to the garden.
>
> We were then lined up against the fence, laying flat on our belly, face down, with our hands behind our heads. They beat us with

---

[72]Human Rights Watch interview with Selman Morina, Golubovac, October 1, 1998.

sticks and stones, and with everything they could find. Those who didn't move were just beaten on the back, but when someone moved they were beaten all over their bodies. We were about 30 centimeters away from each other. I was the third from the entrance. I didn't count the people, but believe there were about fourteen of us.

I was beaten on my back from my buttocks to my neck. I turned once to ask if there was an interrogation inspector whom I could talk to, and a policeman replied, "I am the inspector," and hit me hard in my face. After this I remained quiet. They kept telling us that if we told them who among us belonged to the KLA, they would release all the others. There was no KLA among us, so we didn't know what to do. I was beaten with sticks and kicked, and once I think they hit me with stones. The stick they used to beat us was a shovel handle. We lay there for two or three hours while they beat us and interrogated us. The others were beaten much more than me, because they kept turning their heads to see what was happening.

I believe one policeman executed all of us. A policeman, a new one, came into the garden. I believe one person executed all of us. One man shot us, but the others were around in the garden. We were executed one by one. Each person was fired on twice with a burst from a machine gun. We had nowhere to escape. Some of us were begging to be released. No one tried to get up and escape.

They first shot the second person from the door to the garden, and then they executed the fifth and the sixth one. I cannot remember the order after this. I was the third from the fence, so I know that the person to my right was shot first. They then shot persons close to my left, but not the person immediately next to me, the fourth from the fence, so it must have been the fifth and the sixth. Then, he went down the line, left to right, and then again from right to left.

Each person was shot twice. One person was shot a third time. I heard the police say "One is still alive," and they kicked him once and shot him again. They kicked me too, but I didn't move and then they didn't touch me again. I survived because I remained totally dead. From the time of the bullets, none of us made a noise. Then, I heard them go out in the garden and leave. I heard some more machine gun fire outside the compound, and understood they left. I then attempted to walk home. I first saw my mother and then my wife. I left the garden about ten or fifteen minutes after the police. When I got up, I saw the other men with their faces to the ground and they didn't move.[73]

Human Rights Watch inspected and photographed the wounds on Selman Morina's body after interviewing him on October 1, four days after he had allegedly been shot by the Serbian police. His wounds were consistent with his account. He suffered from a gunshot wound to his upper left thigh, with the entry wound located below the exit wound. The trajectory of this bullet would be consistent with the position of Selman at the time of the summary execution, as he was lying down with his head farthest from the policeman who shot at him. He also had two smaller gun shot wounds on his upper right arm. His back was extensively bruised, consistent with his account of having been beaten on the back prior to the failed execution.

Human Rights Watch researchers visited the site of the executions in the family compound of Adem Hoxhaj in the afternoon of September 29, 1998, after documenting the forest massacre of the Delijaj family in Gornje Obrinje. Adjacent to the bramble fence, Human Rights Watch found sixteen large and small pools of still drying blood and some body tissue. The blood spots ran along the fence, and were consistent with the account of the survivor and witnesses that the execution victims were lying parallel to the fence prior to being shot. Among the blood pools were torn pieces of an identity document.

Approximately eighty shell casings were at the execution site, the vast majority of them scattered on a small one-meter high mound about two meters away from where the execution victims had lain. These casings were identified by the Arms Division of Human Rights Watch as 7.52mm caliber, normally used by the M84 general purpose machine gun. The few smaller casings found amid the blood spots near the fence were identified as 7.62mm caliber, which can be used with a M70B1/B2 (AK-type) or a M72/72AB1 light machine gun. The location of

---

[73]Human Rights Watch interview with Selman Morina, Golubovac, October 1, 1998.

these casings of two different calibers coincides with the first heavy rounds that were fired from the mound by the M84 machine gun, and the later lighter rounds that were fired as the police moved among the bodies, kicking them and firing again at those who moved. Musli and Muje Hoxhaj, who were at Musli Hoxhaj's house during the incident, also described hearing two different bursts of automatic fire, lasting about two minutes or so, before the police quickly left the compound between 4 and 5 p.m. During the day, the police also burned most of the homes in the village and at least one vehicle belonging to Musli Hoxhaj.

After the police left, most of the persons staying at Musli Hoxhaj's compound remained there, too afraid to return home. The gravely wounded Selman Morina initially went to Musli's compound to seek assistance, and was given some apples, milk, and a walking stick before he left again to go to his own home and find his mother and wife (others were too afraid to join him). When he arrived at Musli's compound, Selman told Musli that "they were all killed," and that he was in the line with the others but managed to escape death by feigning death when kicked. After another half hour passed, Musli, Adem, and a third man named Sokol decided to go to Adem's compound. Musli described what they found:

> About one and a half hours after the police left, Adem, Sokol, and myself went on the path through the field to Adem's home. When we got in, there were no police there and we found thirteen dead bodies. Adem turned the bodies around. The bodies were shot in the back. We didn't see if they were beaten, but I know they were shot. They were wearing normal civilian clothes. I saw the thirteen bodies and went crazy.[74]

On Sunday beginning around 12:00 p.m. until approximately 3:00 or 4:00 p.m., the families of the execution victims came to the Golubovac compound to claim the bodies and prepare them for burial in their home villages. According to Musli Hoxhaj and Muje Hoxhaj, six of the men were buried in a suburb of Pločica. The names of those six were:

- Ajet or Rrustem Maloku (name unclear), forty-two, from Pločica;
- Muhamet Maloku, thirty-five, from Pločica;

---

[74]Human Rights Watch interview with Musli Hoxhaj, Golubovac, November 9, 1998.

- Rasim Maloku, thirty-eight, from Pločica;
- Halim Maloku, thirty-seven, from Pločica;
- Ahmet Maloku, between forty-five and fifty, from Pločica;
- Aziz Maloku, forty-five, from Pločica.

Four men were buried in two different graveyards in Golubovac:

- Fazli Hoxhaj, forty-two, from Golubovac;
- Osman Morina, age and origin unknown;
- Remzi Veselaj, thirty-five, from Iglarevo;
- Selmon Gashi, thirty-one, from Pločica.

One was buried in Gjurgjevik:

- Zeqir Berisha, forty, from Gjurgjevik.

Two men whose names were unknown to Musli and Muje Hoxhaj were taken for burial to the villages of Gjurgjevik and Banjica.

The Murder and Burning of Ramadan Hoxha
        The severely burned body of Ramadan Hoxha, a resident of Golubovac, was found on Tuesday, September 29, in the woods above Golubovac. Ramadan had attempted to return to Golubovac from Vučak during the Serb offensive, reportedly to check on his family. When the Golubovac villagers realized he was missing, they began to search the neighboring woods. At about 4 p.m. on Tuesday, Muje Hoxha found Ramadan's body. He described what he found to Human Rights Watch:

> First we found one shoe. Fifteen meters away, we found the
> body of Ramadan totally burned. He was in a crouching
> position against a tree, and only part of his jacket remained
> unburned.[75]

        Muje told Human Rights Watch that he believed Ramadan's body had been burned with gasoline. Human Rights Watch visited the place where

---

        [75]Human Rights Watch interview with Muje Hoxha, Golubovac, November 9, 1998.

Ramadan's body was found, and noticed a small burned place with the remains of partially burned clothes. Human Rights Watch found two shells immediately adjacent to the body which were later determined to be 7.62mm caliber for the M70B1/B2 (AK-type) assault rifle or the M72/72AB1 light machine gun, suggesting that Ramadan might have been executed prior to the burning of his body. A photograph of Ramadan's body has been obtained by Human Rights Watch that shows a corpse blackened by fire, consistent with the accounts of the villagers who helped bury Ramadan. The burns are relatively superficial, consistent with the use of a rapidly burning accelerant.

Human Rights Watch found significant evidence that some type of military or police force had encamped in the area. Mounds of spent bullet casings and the remains of consumed food tins, as well as a used first aid package to dress abdominal injuries with instructions in Serbian, were scattered within one hundred meters of the place where Ramadan's body was found.

The burned remains of villager Ramadan Hoxha being removed from the forest above Golubovac. Human Rights Watch found significant evidence at the site that Hoxha had been executed by Yugoslav forces and his body subsequently burned. Golobovac, September 29, 1998. © 1999 Human Rights Watch.

V. SYSTEMATIC DESTRUCTION OF CIVILIAN PROPERTY

Pločica: A Snapshot of Destruction

Human Rights Watch's first access to Drenica during the offensive was to the village of Pločica on September 26.[76] Shelling continued in the distance and some of the surrounding villages were burning, such as Gornje Obrinje, site of the massacre (see above).

Pločica itself was almost entirely destroyed by the police. One of the buildings in the village was still on fire, a food storage facility holding melons and pumpkins, and many other buildings were still smoldering. Everything at the scene pointed to systematic, premeditated destruction, carried out without any form of resistance by local ethnic Albanians. Most of the homes, some of them century-old stone structures, had been torched and were completely destroyed. Free-standing hay stacks and fences had been burned. Most of the food storage units had also been burned, and valuable possessions such as appliances, satellite dishes, vehicles, and televisions had either been stolen, destroyed, or were severely vandalized. With the exception of a few houses which were not entirely destroyed, personal possessions were strewn everywhere and in most cases burned.

The pattern of destruction of Pločica, duplicated in most of the Drenica villages visited by Human Rights Watch, clearly shows the systematic and premeditated nature of the actions of the Serbian police and Yugoslav Army. It would be impossible to set an entire village on fire without the use of an accelerant. Someone clearly moved through the compound and set individual structures on fire, as it would be impossible due to the distances between homes for the fire, however fierce, to jump from one structure to the next.[77]

The villagers of Pločica were just returning from their hiding places in the nearby forest as Human Rights Watch researchers arrived, and they spoke openly

---

[76]Prior to reaching Pločica, Human Rights Watch researchers had been refused entry to parts of Drenica on two occasions, first by a contingent of Yugoslav Army tanks apparently leaving the area, and second by a police roadblock near the village of Dobro Voda.

[77]One of the notable features of the destruction is that a few homes in the compound were virtually untouched and that others often had a single room which was not burned. Local villagers and Priština-based activists speculated that the goal of the Yugoslav forces was not to completely destroy the villages, but rather to create a humanitarian crisis in which civilians would be focused on survival and rebuilding their ruined lives rather than providing support to the KLA. Leaving some homes untouched also helps breed mistrust and jealousy within the community.

about their plight. They said the previous day, September 25, they had heard shelling and shooting near their compound around 9:00 a.m. and fled to the nearby woods without their possessions. Without warning, they said, tanks approached and shelled the village, and they saw policemen following the tanks. According to the villagers, Pločica was intact when they fled and there was no KLA presence in the village. Human Rights Watch saw no evidence that the KLA had been in the village, such as the remains of trenches or other defensive positions.

Villagers told Human Rights Watch that they watched from a nearby vantage point and saw the police enter their village around 11 a.m. on September 25. Qamil Kryeziu, a villager from nearby Mlečane who had fled to Pločica one month before when his home was attacked, told Human Rights Watch that the villagers had spent the night in the forest at a place called Vučak, and that the police had surrounded the place around 11:30 a.m. on September 26.[78] According to Kryeziu, the police told the villagers to raise their hands and come out of the forest. The police detained the villagers for about an hour, and then told them to gather their belongings and return to their homes.

Human Rights Watch walked through Pločica for several hours, interviewing villagers as they returned to their ruined homes. During the entire period of time, the two researchers did not find a single bullet casing or any other evidence that active combat had taken place at the compound. The burned homes did not have any bullet or shell damage, and thus did not ignite during combat. There was no evidence in or around the village of any KLA presence, and no part of the village appeared to have been prepared for combat through the digging of trenches or sandbagging of homes (a practice observed by Human Rights Watch in other villages with a KLA presence). While the KLA did control the Drenica area prior to the offensive, and it is possible that KLA soldiers may have moved through the village, the evidence found by Human Rights Watch strongly indicates that the village had offered no resistance, and had been burned after being abandoned by the local population.

The only military equipment found by Human Rights Watch around the compound were two dozen spent 82 mm mortar casings used by the M6, M69, or M31 mortar launchers in a nearby field. The mortar launchers had left deep imprints in the soil, and it was possible to determine that the mortars had been fired away from Pločica in the direction of the forest, perhaps toward nearby Golubovac.

---

[78]Human Rights Watch interview with Qamil Kryeziu, Pločica, September 26, 1998.

A villager of Pločica in front of his burning food shed containing squashes, melons and other winter foods. The villagers had been forced to flee due to shelling the day before and returned to find their village systematically destroyed. September 26, 1998. © 1999 Human Rights Watch.

A villager from Pločica sitting in front of the still-smoldering remains of his destroyed home. September 26, 1998. © 1999 Human Rights Watch.

A member of the Delijaj family at his destroyed food storage shed in Likovac. The bags of flour had been ripped and their contents strewn about. Likovac, November 1998. © 1999 Human Rights Watch.

Villages on fire in Drenica, as seen from the village of Pločica on September 26, 1998. Heavy artillery reverberated in the background. © 1999 Human Rights Watch.

Serbian nationalist graffiti, including the cyrillic cross, painted on a destroyed
building in the Drenica region of Kosovo. November 1998. © 1999 Human
Rights Watch.

The information on the mortar shells indicates that they are of Yugoslav manufacture.

The Larger Picture: Destruction of Civilian Objects in Kosovo
Throughout Kosovo, Yugoslav forces have repeatedly and deliberately destroyed civilian property and objects essential to the survival of the civilian population. Clear and substantiated evidence exists that the vast majority of the destroyed properties were systematically burned by Serb police after the towns were abandoned by local villagers.

The experiences related by people from various villages that have been destroyed in Kosovo present a strikingly similar pattern. First, a village was surrounded by Yugoslav forces, sometimes after fighting with the KLA, and soon thereafter shelling of the village began, usually by the army. Villagers would flee into the forest to escape the shelling, leaving the village abandoned except for those unable to flee. Time and time again, villagers would tell Human Rights Watch how they watched from a nearby vantage point as their village was systematically looted and burned by Serbian police. The testimonies of these witnesses is corroborated by Human Rights Watch's own observations: police forces were repeatedly seen entering areas as military forces were withdrawing. Although the main forces of the army have generally been less involved in the most egregious atrocities committed in Kosovo—maybe because they have focused on destructive long-range bombardment rather than close combat—the pattern of operation described confirms close coordination between the Yugoslav Army and the various police units involved in the Kosovo conflict.

The destruction was not limited to civilian homes. In Mališevo, Dečan and other larger towns, Yugoslav authorities looted and destroyed entire commercial districts, painting "OBK" and "UQK" (Serbian spellings (and misspellings) for UÇK, the Albanian acronym for the Kosovo Liberation Army), "Srbija" (the Serbian spelling for Serbia), the nationalist cyrillic cross, or nationalist slogans such as "Srbija do Tokija" ("Serbia to Tokyo") on destroyed buildings.

A journalist told Human Rights Watch he saw Serbian police filling two-liter plastic containers with gasoline from a tanker truck to burn down a shopping mall in Mališevo. When he returned to the area a short while later, the shopping mall was up in flames:

> Toward the end of August, we were about five kilometers outside Mališevo when we saw a gas tanker. We could smell the gasoline from the tanker. There were uniformed policemen

filling two-liter plastic bottles from the tanker. When we got into Mališevo, there were raging flames and fresh fires. It was a strip of stores which was burning. Mališevo had been abandoned at this stage for about a week, and there was no fighting at all.[79]

In many areas, Serbian police targeted food supplies and other essentials. Human Rights Watch researchers saw cattle that had been killed and left dead in the fields in many areas of Kosovo, many had been shot, especially in Drenica following the government offensive, which suggests that they were killed on purpose to deprive local civilians of their use. Many villagers complained that their food supplies and cattle fodder had been looted by police, and Human Rights Watch found significant evidence that food supplies had been specifically targeted for destruction. Free-standing hay stacks, granaries, and other storage facilities were often burned down. In Likovac, Human Rights Watch researchers were shown the remains of a storage shed that had held a significant amount of flour for human consumption, and observed that almost all the bags had been torn and their contents strewn about. In Dobro Voda, a recently returned family complained to Human Rights Watch that all their food supplies had been stolen, and that their sheep had been killed and consumed by Serb police headquartered at the local school building, which was destroyed by police as they departed. Looting was also common in most destroyed villages, and many villagers told Human Rights Watch that the police had stolen valuable goods from their homes. On September 26, Human Rights Watch directly observed two blue uniformed policemen in Mlečane carrying boxes of goods out of private homes.

UNHCR found that water wells in Dobrosevac had been intentionally polluted with dead animals and garbage,[80] a practice confirmed in other areas by humanitarian organizations. R. Jeffrey Smith wrote about widespread poisoning of civilian wells in Kosovo in the *Washington Post*:

Most of the poisonings appear to have occurred shortly before Yugoslavia withdrew many of its forces under threat of NATO air strikes in October, allowing thousands of refugees to return home. Since then, refugees in at least 58 villages throughout

[79]Human Rights Watch interview with Justin Brown, *Christian Science Monitor* reporter, Priština, September 23, 1998.
[80]UNHCR briefing notes, October 23, 1998.

Kosovo have informed foreign aid organizations that their wells contain dead dogs, chickens, horses, garbage, fuel oil, flour, detergent, paint and other contaminants. Although many of these reports have not been confirmed, a few aid groups that have begun testing and cleaning residential wells in villages say that they have found evidence to confirm the allegations.[81]

R. Jeffrey Smith described visiting a village and being shown a well in which the remains of a dog had been found. He concluded that the poisonings could not have been accidental:

This dog could not have wandered into the well. It had a concrete cover on it .... These things don't wander into the wells accidentally. These wells are usually, you know, placed in very obvious locations. A lot of them are covered. Anything that you find at the bottom of the well other than water has been put there by somebody.[82]

Because of the systemic destruction carried out throughout Kosovo by the Yugoslav forces, many civilians in Kosovo face a harsh winter inside homes that had been largely destroyed, their provisions for the winter looted and burned.

Paddy Ashdown, leader of the Liberal Party in the United Kingdom, during a visit to the Drenica region on September 26, personally observed the methods of destruction used by the Yugoslav forces and wrote about his observations in the *Guardian*:

First comes the ultimatum, delivered by the Serb police. "Give up your weapons or we will destroy your village."

After the deadline comes the shelling. Heavy artillery and 120-millimeter mortars and heavy caliber machine guns and T55 tanks. The weapons of total war, against defenseless civilians. One after the other, I watched them.

---

[81]R. Jeffrey Smith, "Poisoned Wells Plague Towns All Over Kosovo," *Washington Post*, December 9, 1998.

[82]National Public Radio, *All Things Considered*, December 9, 1998, 8:22 p.m. ET.

Next come the soldier looters with heavy articulated lorries, into which are loaded the meager valuables of a peasant population. And finally the soldiers who systematically burn the houses one after the other up the valley. I watched them; three days after the Security Council had passed a resolution saying this must stop and at the same time as the Yugoslav government had assured the world that it had stopped. I counted 17 villages in flames and countless individual farmhouses.

I spoke to the terrified human flotsam of this medieval barbarism.[83]

A number of the humanitarian aid organizations currently operating in Kosovo are cooperating on a survey to assess the damage caused during the fighting in Kosovo.[84] Their preliminary results provide compelling testimony to the widespread nature of destruction. The survey assessed 285 villages, of which 210 had been affected by the conflict. In the 210 affected villages with an estimated pre-conflict population of 350,000 persons, twenty-eight percent of the homes—9,809 out of a total of 35,185 homes—had been completely destroyed. Another fifteen percent of the homes (5,112 homes) had severe damage, while an additional 6,017 homes sustained moderate to minor damage, leaving only forty percent of the homes in the affected regions undamaged.[85]

The scale of the destruction of civilian property and of objects essential to the survival of the civilian population, clearly visible throughout the area of the Yugoslav offensive, provides indisputable proof that the destruction was carried out as a matter of state policy, and cannot be viewed as the actions of rogue soldiers or policemen. As such, responsibility for these systematic violations of the laws of war and crimes against humanity lies with the top of the command structure of

---

[83]Paddy Ashdown, "Milosevic tells me no one is left living in the open in Kosovo. I tell him his officials are lying," *Guardian* (London), September 30, 1998.

[84]Humanitarian organizations working on the survey include: Save the Children Fund (SCF); Danish Refugee Council (DRC); Catholic Relief Services (CRS); Medecins Sans Frontieres (MSF); Swiss Disaster Relief (SDR); International Rescue Committee (IRC); Mercy Corps International (MCI); InterSOS; OXFAM; WFP; Children's Aid Direct (CAD); UNICEF; World Vision (WVI); UNHCR; CARE International; and Doctors of the World (DOW).

[85]*IDP/Shelter Survey Kosovo: Joint Assessment in 20 Municipalities*, released by UNHCR Priština, dated November 12, 1998.

The mosque of Gornje Obrinje, destroyed by Yugoslav forces during the offensive. Human Rights Watch found mosques throughout Kosovo which were destroyed. November 1998. © 1999 Human Rights Watch.

The mosque at Gornje Obrinje, destroyed during the Yugoslav offensive.
November 1998. © 1999 Human Rights Watch.

A school outside Likovac, destroyed by Yugoslav forces. November 1998. © 1999 Human Rights Watch.

The inside of a destroyed school near Golubovac. Schools for ethnic Albanians throughout Kosovo were targeted for destruction by Yugoslav forces. November 1998. © 1999 Human Rights Watch.

VI. THE RESPONSE OF THE YUGOSLAV AUTHORITIES

Since the beginning of the Kosovo conflict, the Yugoslav government has engaged in a systematic campaign of propaganda and disinformation presenting a view of the conflict that is clearly at odds with the reality on the ground. Misinformation about the conflict has served to whip up xenophobic nationalism and fears of an international anti-Serb conspiracy, a central pillar of President Milošević's rule.

On September 28, 1998, before the atrocities revealed in this report were uncovered, Serbia's Prime Minister Mirko Marjanovic gave a victory speech:

> Today there is peace in Kosovo Metohija.[87] Life in Kosovo Metohija has returned to normal. The Republic of Serbia has thwarted the secessionists' attempts to realize their intentions through terror. The terrorist gangs have been destroyed ... Serbia has once again shown that it is capable of resolving its problems alone, with full respect for the democratic countries' principles and standards regarding human, civil and minority rights.[88]

The response of the Yugoslav authorities to reports of the atrocities in Gornje Obrinje and Golubovac was along similar lines. The spokesman of the Ministry of Interior Affairs of Serbia, Colonel Božidar Filić, denied that the police had been responsible for the atrocities, stating that "MUP [police] forces did not undertake any actions against civilians in the village of Gornje Obrinje," and that "all actions undertaken by the police in Kosovo were aimed exclusively against terrorists."[89]

Most news programs on the official Serbian television (RTS), which is tightly controlled by the government, suggested that the Gornje Obrinje massacre had either been staged by Western media or by ethnic Albanian "terrorists." The RTS evening news even suggested that a widely publicized photograph of

---

undefined towns, villages, dwellings, or buildings."

[87]"Kosovo Metohija" is the official Serbian term for Kosovo.

[88]Quoted in Bob Dole, "How Convenient," *Wall Street Journal*, September 30, 1998.

[89]*Tanjug*, September 30, 1998.

eighteen-month-old Valmir Delijaj was actually a photograph of a doll, and the reporter held up what he claimed was a "similar" doll smeared with blood. Western television sometimes did not show human corpses in its coverage of the massacres out of consideration for the sensitivity of viewers, but the RTS news argued that this showed that reports about the massacre had been fabricated. Pictures of the corpses that ran in the international media, including the front page of the *New York Times*, as well as such local papers as the Albanian-language *Koha Ditore*, were conveniently ignored. Human Rights Watch researchers gave interviews about their findings to the independent Serbia media, such as the Beta news agency and Radio B92, as well as to numerous international journalists, but were never approached by any of the state-run media outlets, even though those journalists were aware of Human Rights Watch's presence in Priština.

Serbian political leaders also claimed that the massacres had been staged by the Western media and the KLA to justify NATO bombing. Vojislav Šešelj, leader of the Serbian Radical Party and deputy prime minister of Serbia, claimed that the massacre at Gornje Obrinje "was orchestrated in the West by those same countries in order to create legal grounds for the U.N. Security Council to authorize the bombing of Serbia."[90] He continued with his familiar refrain of a vast conspiracy against the Serbian people:

> All propaganda services and agencies for waging the propaganda war of the Western powers have joined forces in an orchestrated campaign against Serbia, the Serb people, and the FRY.
>
> What we saw in Kosovo, in the village of Gornje Obrinje, is identical to the promulgation of false reports on the events at the [Sarajevo] Markale market place, Vase Miskina Street, and the Partisan Cemetery in Sarajevo, when Alija Izetbegovic had his own civilians killed in order to impute those killings to the Serbs.
>
> [Those responsible are] the Shiptar[91] terrorists, because they were militarily defeated by the police and army, who used the

---

[90]"Šešelj says Kosovo massacre fabricated in order to bomb Serbs," *Beta*, October 1, 1998.

[91]"Shiptar," which means "an Albanian" in the Albanian language ("Shqiptar"), is a derogatory word for Albanians when used by Serbs.

most perfidious and corrupt means, sacrificed their own people, and called up the foreign diplomats and correspondents...[92]

The official RTS television attributed similar statements to Vuk Drasković, head of the Serbian Renewal Movement Party (SPO) and a Deputy Prime Minister of Serbia since mid-January, who reportedly stated that:

Logic and all the available facts lead to the conclusion that the Albanian civilians were killed by those whose propaganda and strategic interest would be served by such a crime. The Albanian terrorists had every reason to stage the massacre against their compatriots and thus push their atrocities [against Serbs] in Klečka and Glodjane aside, simultaneously rousing anti-Serb emotions and triggering NATO pact aggression against Serbia.[93]

---

[92]"Šešelj says Kosovo massacre fabricated in order to bomb Serbs," *Beta*, October 1, 1998.

[93]"Party leader says 'logic' indicates Kosovo rebels carried out massacre," *RTS TV*, October 1, 1998, 17:30 gmt. Klečka and Glodjane refer to two sites where ethnic Albanians are accused of committing execution-style killings. Many questions surround the Klečka allegations, but the deaths of thirty-four people, ethnic Albanians and Serbs whose bodies were found in a lake near Glodjane can be attributed more directly to the KLA. For details on abuses by the KLA, see the Human Rights Watch report, "Humanitarian Law Violations in Kosovo," October 1998.

VII. THE ROLE OF THE INTERNATIONAL COMMUNITY

International Response to the Massacres

Virtually all relevant governments and international organizations responded to the Gornje Obrinje and Golubovac massacres with outrage. As with every other atrocity thus far in the Kosovo conflict, however, verbal condemnations and threats were not followed by serious measures to ensure that such atrocities would not happen again. Another massacre, in Račak on January 15, 1999, in which as many as forty-five ethnic Albanians were tortured and summarily executed by Yugoslav forces indicates that President Milošević feels free to continue his unlawful attacks on civilians.[94]

The pattern is familiar. The international community expresses moral outrage about an atrocity and promises "decisive action," including a possible military intervention. Milošević responds with a temporary pull-back of his forces and some vague commitments. But no one is willing to take the necessary steps to hold Milosovic to his commitments.

The most common refrain is the "serious threat" of NATO action against Yugoslav government forces or installations, most likely in the form of air strikes. Western governments, especially the U.S., have devised ever more creative methods—NATO activization orders, the mobilization of troops, impressive air exercises, assertive statements, or leaks to the press—to convince the Western public and the Yugoslav government of their readiness to use force.

But so far, measures by the international community have been weakly enforced, and sometimes rescinded when Milošević makes concessions on actions that he should not have undertaken in the first place. While the West characterizes these measures as strong steps against a dictator, the abuses continue.

The Yugoslav government's violations of international ultimatums aimed at ending the abuses in Kosovo are frequent and blatant. The attacks on Gornje Obrinje and Golubovac, for instance, took place three days after the U.N. Security Council adopted Resolution 1199 (1998), which demanded that the Yugoslav security forces immediately "cease all action... affecting the civilian population and order the withdrawal of security units used for civilian repression."[95] But the Security Council, itself stymied by the potential vetoes of Russia and China, did not take any serious steps in response to the Yugoslav government's intransigence.

---

[94]See Appendix A, *Yugoslav Government War Crimes in Račak*, Human Rights Watch, January 1999.
[95]U.N. Security Council Resolution 1199 (1998).

The Holbrooke-Milošević Agreement and the OSCE Kosovo Verification Mission (KVM)

When the Gornje Obrinje and Golubovac atrocities hit the Western press, the U.S. government sent Richard Holbrooke, White House special envoy to the Balkans, to Belgrade for negotiations with Yugoslav President Milošević. After protracted discussions, Holbrooke announced that an agreement had been reached, although no official text was released. The agreement included four essential points: the Federal Republic of Yugoslavia agreed to abide by the conditions of U.N. Security Council Resolution 1199 and to allow NATO monitoring in Yugoslav airspace to ensure compliance, to permit the deployment in Kosovo of a 2,000-person OSCE unarmed civilian "verification team," and to engage in a political dialogue with ethnic Albanian leaders over the political status of Kosovo.[96]

Shortly thereafter, the OSCE mission began to take shape, headed by a U.S. diplomat, William Walker, former U.S. ambassador to El Salvador. By January, the Kosovo Verification Mission (KVM) had approximately 800 people on the ground with branch offices in most of Kosovo's larger towns. While the KVM has been successful in putting out small fires, such as negotiating the release of prisoners, it was not able to halt an escalation of hostilities in early 1999. A group of verifiers watched from a ridge as government forces fought with the KLA in Račak on January 15, shortly before Yugoslav forces tortured and summarily executed as many as forty-five ethnic Albanian civilians in the village.

On the positive side, KVM includes a human rights department that is actively collecting information on human rights abuses committed by all sides in

---

[96]The only announcement from the Yugoslav government came through the Serbian President Milan Milutinović in his report to the Serbian government on October 13. The report presents the OSCE mission and stresses the government's intention to resolve the Kosovo conflict peacefully and through dialogue as long as Kosovo remains within "the framework of Serbia." Point 10 of statement also said:

> Not one person will be criminally prosecuted before government courts for criminal acts in connection with the conflict in Kosovo, except for those crimes against humanity and international law as foreseen in Chapter 16 of the Federal Criminal Law. With a goal of ensuring complete openness, the government will allow complete and unhindered access by foreign experts (including pathologists) who will cooperate with government investigators.

Neither of these promises, to halt criminal prosecutions in Kosovo or to allow unhindered access by foreign experts, has been kept by the Serbian government.

the conflict, although its reporting has not been made public. Ambassador Walker openly condemned the attack on civilians in Račak, which he correctly blamed directly on Yugoslav government forces. (See Appendix A)

The Work of the International Criminal Tribunal for the Former Yugoslavia
Human rights organizations can document the abuses taking place in Kosovo, and the international community can take steps to bring these abuses to an end. But the only institution that has been entrusted by the international community to prosecute the persons responsible for violations of humanitarian law is the International Criminal Tribunal for the Former Yugoslavia (ICTY). The role of the ICTY is of crucial importance, as the prosecution of those who commit atrocities is likely to have a significant deterrent effect in addition to upholding the principles of international justice.

ICTY's jurisdiction over war crimes committed in Kosovo under its mandate as set out in U.N. Security Council resolution 827 is undisputable and has been repeatedly reaffirmed by the U.N. Security Council in its resolutions on Kosovo,[97] as well as by the tribunal itself.[98]

The Yugoslav authorities have refused to accept the jurisdiction of the ICTY, and have frustrated the work of ICTY investigators in Kosovo by refusing to grant them visas and barring them from carrying out investigations. Only a few ICTY investigators have been able to gain access to Kosovo, and even they have been formally prohibited by the Yugoslav authorities from interviewing persons or gathering evidence. The Yugoslav authorities base their refusal to cooperate with the ICTY on their view that the conflict in Kosovo is an internal dispute with

---

[97] U.N. Security Council Resolution 827 established the ICTY "for the sole purpose of prosecuting persons responsible for serious violations of international humanitarian law committed in the territory of the former Yugoslavia between 1 January 1991 and a date to be determined by the Security Council upon the restoration of peace..." Kosovo is located inside the territory of the former Yugoslavia, and the Security Council has not yet determined a date on which the jurisdiction of the ICTY will expire.

In Resolution 1160, adopted on March 31, 1998, the U.N. Security Council "[u]rges the Office of the Prosecutor of the International Tribunal established pursuant to Resolution 827 (1993) of 25 May 1993 to begin gathering information related to the violence in Kosovo that may fall within its jurisdiction, and notes that the authorities of the Federal Republic of Yugoslavia have an obligation to co-operate with the Tribunal...".

In Resolution 1199, adopted on September 23, 1998, the U.N. Security Council noted "the communication by the Prosecutor [of the ICTY] to the Contact Group on 7 July 1998, expressing the view that the situation in Kosovo represents an armed conflict within the terms of the mandate of the Tribunal," and called upon all parties "to co-operate fully with the Prosecutor [of the ICTY] in the investigation of possible violations within the jurisdiction of the Tribunal."

On October 1, 1998, following an emergency session of the U.N. Security Council to discuss the initial reports of the massacres documented in this report, the U.N. Security Council again reaffirmed the jurisdiction of the ICTY: "Council Members recalled the role of the International Criminal Tribunal for Yugoslavia, which is empowered to investigate violations of international humanitarian law in Kosovo."

[98]The International Criminal Tribunal for the Former Yugoslavia press statement, "The Prosecutor's Statement Regarding the Tribunal's Jurisdiction Over Kosovo," The Hague, March 10, 1998; The International Criminal Tribunal for the Former Yugoslavia press statement, "Communication from the Prosecutor to the Contact Group Members," The Hague, July 7, 1998.

"terrorists," a view repeatedly rejected by the ICTY, the U.N. Security Council, and other international actors.[99]

In early October, immediately following the initial reports of the atrocities documented in this report, Yugoslav authorities first denied visas to ICTY investigators. According to a statement by the ICTY's Office of the Prosecutor:

> Up until the last few weeks, the Prosecutor has been undertaking investigations in relation to the events in Kosovo without any obstruction from the Belgrade authorities. A team has just returned from Kosovo and it was the Prosecutor's intention to supplement this team with other investigators. That has not been possible because for the first time the Belgrade authorities had not issued visas in time for these other investigators to travel to Yugoslavia. ... [T]he representatives of the Foreign Ministry indicated that the official position of the Federal Republic of Yugoslavia (FRY) regarding the Tribunal and Kosovo is that the Tribunal has no jurisdiction to conduct investigations in Kosovo and the Tribunal will not be allowed to do so.[100]

The October 12 agreement between Yugoslav President Slobodan Milošević and U.S. envoy Richard Holbrooke did not contain a recognition of the ICTY's jurisdiction, although Milosovic did agree to abide by Security Council Resolution 1199 (which in turn refers to ICTY jurisdiction) and to increase access for ICTY investigators to Kosovo—a promise soon broken.[101] Zoran Knežević, the Yugoslav Minister of Justice, later reiterated the government's position that the October 12 agreement does not require Belgrade to recognize the jurisdiction of the ICTY, and stated that the ICTY "has no jurisdiction over Kosovo, not according to any international document."[102]

---

[99] The Kosovo conflict has reached the level of an internal armed conflict, so that, at the very least, Common Article 3 of the Geneva Conventions applies. For a full discussion of the relevant international law, see the Human Rights Watch report "Humanitarian Law Violations in Kosovo," October 1998.

[100]Statement by the Office of the Prosecutor, "The Prosecutor does not accept the refusal by the FRY to allow Kosovo investigations," October 7, 1998.

[101]Jane Perlez, "Milosevic Accepts Kosovo Monitors, Averting Attack," *New York Times*, October 14, 1998.

[102]"Yugoslav justice minister denies Hague Tribunal jurisdiction in Kosovo," *Associated Press*, October 30, 1998. Minister Knezevic made a similar statement on October 15, stating that the Belgrade government does not recognize the jurisdiction of the

On November 5, 1998, Louise Arbour, chief prosecutor for the ICTY, and Judge Gabrielle Kirk McDonald, president of the ICTY, were forced to cancel a proposed mission to Kosovo after the Yugoslav government granted the team restricted visas that were only valid for seven days and did not permit travel to Kosovo. The decision to refuse the visa requests was based on the refusal of the FRY government to recognize the jurisdiction of the ICTY over Kosovo, as explained in a letter from the FRY Ambassador to Chief Prosecutor Arbour:

> As you have already been informed, the Federal Republic of Yugoslavia does not accept any investigations of ICTY in Kosovo and Metohija generally, nor during your stay in the FR of Yugoslavia."[103]

Judge Kirk McDonald characterized the refusal to grant the proper visas as the actions "of a rogue state that holds the international rule of law in contempt," and later wrote to the U.N. Security Council to ask for "measures which are sufficiently compelling to bring the Federal Republic of Yugoslavia into the fold of law-abiding nations."[104]

The U.N. Security Council passed Resolution 1207 on November 17, 1998, dealing specifically with the noncompliance of the Federal Republic of Yugoslavia with the ICTY. However, the language of the resolution relating to Kosovo was relatively weak, possibly in order to avert a veto from Russia or China. China abstained from the vote on the basis that the ICTY "does not have the right to interfere in the internal affairs" of Yugoslavia.[105]

It is not difficult to ascertain why Belgrade refuses to recognize the jurisdiction of the ICTY. Serious violations of the laws of war have been committed in Kosovo, and the officials responsible for these abuses are liable to indictment and prosecution by the tribunal. The actions of the Yugoslav authorities

---

ICTY but would allow ICTY investigators access to Kosovo. "Belgrade does not recognize ICTY jurisdiction in Kosovo: Minister," *Agence France Presse*, October 15, 1998. Such access was never provided.

[103]"Statement by Justice Louise Arbour, Prosecutor of the ICTY," November 5, 1998.

[104]Letter of Gabrielle Kirk McDonald, Judge President of the ICTY, to the U.N. Security Council; "War Crimes Court cancels mission to Yugoslavia," *Agence France Presse*, November 5, 1998; Elena Becatoros, "U.S. Envoy sees progress in Kosovo peace efforts," *Associated Press*, November 5, 1998.

[105]"UN Security Council Demands Belgrade Cooperation on Kosovo," *Agence France Presse*, November 17, 1998.

have indeed been successful in limiting the work of the ICTY in Kosovo, and crucial evidence of war crimes may have been lost or tampered with as the ICTY attempts to negotiate access. Government obstacles, for example, preventing ICTY personnel from visiting the Gornje Obrinje and Golubovac sites prior to the burial of the bodies made it much more difficult to secure important forensic evidence and eyewitness testimonies. For its part, the ICTY Prosecutor has correctly asserted that the question of the tribunal's jurisdiction over crimes committed in Kosovo should be resolved in court by tribunal judges, not asserted by Yugoslav authorities as a ban to an investigation.[106] Leaving the question of jurisdiction to later resolution in court, the Prosecutor has undertaken that "[t]he granting of access to Kosovo to [her] Office for investigative purposes will not constitute an admission by the FRY that the ICTY has any jurisdiction in this matter."[107]

Many of the witnesses interviewed by Human Rights Watch for this report expressed a desire to cooperate with the ICTY, and were often living in great fear because no steps had been taken by the international community to ensure their safety.[108] Only through concerted international action, based on clear benchmarks for compliance, and decisive steps in the face of noncompliance, will the ICTY be able effectively to carry out its vitally important mandate. Such political commitment by the international community to the work of the ICTY has been sorely lacking.

The Work of Forensic Teams in Kosovo
In addition to the investigations into humanitarian law violations in Kosovo being carried out by the ICTY and human rights organizations, there is a need for specialized forensic investigations. As the experience in other parts of the Balkans has demonstrated, professional forensic investigations can assist in determining the time, circumstances, and causes of death. Many of the testimonies gathered by Human Rights Watch describe the execution-style murders of captives, such as the killing with an axe of two persons at the Hysenaj compound of Gornje Obrinje, witnessed directly by an elderly woman. Forensic evidence helps to support such witness testimony, and can have additional probative value: for example, a person killed through multiple blows from an axe is more likely to have

---

[106]ICTY Press Release, "Kosovo: Statement by Justice Louise Arbour, Prosecutor of the ICTY," January 16, 1999.
[107]ICTY Press Release, "Press Statement from the Prosecutor regarding Kosovo Investigation," January 20, 1999.
[108]The international community did, however, play an important role in evacuating Selmon Morina, the sole survivor of the summary executions carried out in Golubovac.

been the victim of an execution-style killing than someone killed by a long-distance bullet.

The Yugoslav authorities have effectively prevented forensic scientists from carrying out credible and useful investigations into allegations of atrocities committed by Yugoslav forces. Physicians for Human Rights (PHR), a professional association of forensic scientists applied for twelve visas on March 13, 1998, to conduct forensic investigations into the deaths of eighty persons killed in Drenica during the February 1998 police actions in Kosovo. The Yugoslav authorities responded six weeks later, stating that they would be willing to grant three visas to U.S. members of PHR, contingent on their participation with other investigators designated by the Yugoslav government. These conditions were considered unacceptable to PHR, which characterized them as attempts to "stymie any serious investigation into the Kosovo killings."[109]

Instead of allowing independent investigations, the Yugoslav authorities proceeded to conduct their own investigation into several atrocities that the government claimed had been carried out by the KLA. However, the manner of the exhumations and investigations carried out at Klečka, Glodjane, and Volujak raises serious concerns about the preservation of evidence.[110] A Human Rights Watch researcher was present at the Volujak exhumations of four bodies, and clearly observed the lack of scientific procedures followed by the untrained persons at the scene. For example, body parts were removed from the scene before entire corpses were exhumed and photographed. No forensic experts were present at the exhumation; such exhumations are more likely to destroy crucial evidence than produce anything substantial. While the KLA has been directly implicated in some serious abuses, especially summary executions near Glodjane, serious questions have also been raised about the validity of the information presented by the Yugoslav authorities, especially about the Klečka site. This underlines the importance of an independent and credible forensic investigation into all allegations of atrocities in Kosovo.

Following the Holbrooke-Milošević agreement, an independent forensic team from Helsinki, Finland, was invited by Belgrade to support the work of Yugoslav authorities investigating KLA atrocities. The Finnish team, sponsored by the European Union, accepted the invitation but insisted on a mandate also to

---

[109]PHR Press Release, "On the Eve of Contact Group Meeting, Medical Group Accuses Yugoslav Government of Stymying Investigation into Kosovo Killing," dated April 28, 1998.

[110]For information on KLA abuses in Glodjane and Klečka, see the Human Rights Watch report, "Humanitarian Law Violations in Kosovo," pp. 77-78.

conduct investigations into allegations of atrocities by Yugoslav forces, particularly Gornje Obrinje, Golubovac, and Orahovac. After lengthy negotiations between the Finnish government and the Belgrade authorities, the Finnish team was able to get a promise from Belgrade that it would be allowed to investigate six sites, including three sites of suspected KLA atrocities (Klečka, Glodjane, and Volujak) and three sites of suspected atrocities by Yugoslav forces (Gornje Obrinje, Golubovac, and Orahovac).

The Finnish team conducted investigations at the Klečka and Volujak sites without interference from the Yugoslav government or the KLA. When the Finnish forensic team attempted to reach the Gornje Obrinje site for a planned exhumation on December 10, 1998, a series of incidents with the Yugoslav authorities prevented them from reaching the site. A Serb court official, Priština investigative judge Danica Marinković, and two members of a Belgrade-based forensic team insisted they had the right to accompany the Finnish team, and that the Finnish team could not work on exhumations without their presence.[111] In addition, a heavily armed contingent of Serb police in armored personnel carriers (APCs) insisted on accompanying the forensic team to Gornje Obrinje, which was then located in an area under KLA control. During the two-hour negotiation aimed at resolving the incident, the police repeatedly attempted to shelter themselves from possible KLA attack by moving their APC vehicles behind the diplomatic vehicles of the European KDOM contingent in which the Finnish scientists were traveling. In addition, a plainclothes policeman at the scene violated the diplomatic immunity of Finnish Ambassador for Human Rights Timothy Lahelma, by opening the door of his diplomatic car, grabbing Ambassador Lahelma's camera, and removing the film. The KLA made it clear that it would not allow the Serbian police accompanying the Finnish team to travel through the territory under KLA control. The Finnish forensic team, after consultation with European diplomats, decided to abandon its attempt to reach Gornje Obrinje rather than risk an armed confrontation

---

[111]The choice of judge Danica Marinković to accompany the Finnish team was interpreted as deliberately provocative by many ethnic Albanians, as this particular judge has been tied to a number of torture of ethnic Albanians in custody, sometimes leading to deaths in detention. See Human Rights Watch, *Persecution Persists: Human Rights Violations in Kosovo* (December 1996) and Human Rights Watch, "*Detentions and Abuse in Kosovo,*" December 1998. Marinković also served as an investigative judge in the Klečka case, interrogating two ethnic Albanian suspects in front of television cameras. The allegations of KLA atrocities at Klečka continue to be a matter of dispute.

between their police escorts and the KLA.[112] Yugoslav authorities continue to insist that the Finnish team can only carry out investigations in cooperation with their Belgrade-based counterparts and a local court official, and that a police escort is essential to ensure the safety of the Yugoslav authorities.

---

[112]Human Rights Watch telephone interview with Ambassador Timothy Lahelma, December 11, 1998.

FOR RELEASE JANUARY 29, 1999

For further information, contact:
In New York: Fred Abrahams (212) 216-1270
In Brussels: Jean-Paul Marthoz (322) 732-2009
In London: Urmi Shah (44-171) 713-1995
Check: www.hrw.org/hrw/campaigns/kosovo98/index.htm

Human Rights Watch investigation finds:

Yugoslav Forces Guilty of War Crimes in Račak, Kosovo

(January 29, New York) — Human Rights Watch today categorically rejected Yugoslav government claims that the victims of the January 15 attack on Račak were either Kosovo Liberation Army soldiers killed in combat, or civilians caught in crossfire.

After a detailed investigation, the organization accused Serbian special police forces and the Yugoslav army of indiscriminately attacking civilians, torturing detainees, and committing summary executions. The evidence suggests that government forces had direct orders to kill village inhabitants over the age of fifteen.

The killing of forty-five ethnic Albanian civilians has provoked an apparent shift in western policy toward Kosovo, which the Contact Group is meeting in London today to discuss.

A report in the Washington Post yesterday provided excerpts from telephone conversations between Serbian Interior Ministry General Sreten Lukic and Yugoslav Deputy Prime Minister Nikola Sainovic, who clearly ordered government security forces to "go in heavy" in Račak. The two officials later discussed ways that the killings might be covered up to avoid international condemnation.

Human Rights Watch conducted separate interviews in Kosovo with fourteen witnesses to the attack, many of whom are hiding out of fear for their lives, as well as with foreign journalists and observers who visited Račak on January 16. Together, the testimonies suggest a well planned and executed attack by government forces on civilians in Račak, where the KLA had a sizable presence and had conducted some ambushes on police patrols.

As has happened on numerous occasions in the Kosovo conflict, once the KLA retreated, government forces moved in and committed atrocities against the residents of the village. While it is possible that some residents may have defended their homes in the morning, most were clearly not involved in any armed resistance. At least twenty-three people were summarily executed by the police while offering no resistance — a clear violation of the laws of war, and a crime punishable by the International Criminal Tribunal for the former Yugoslavia (ICTY).

Villagers told consistent stories of how government forces rounded up, tortured, and then apparently executed the twenty-three ethnic Albanians on a hill outside of the village. Two witnesses interviewed by Human Rights Watch saw these men being beaten by the police and then taken off in the direction of the hill. Local villagers, foreign journalists, and diplomatic observers who saw the bodies the next day said that the victims had been shot from close range, most of them in the head; some of them appeared to have been shot while running away. Four men are known to have survived.

Eighteen other people were killed inside Račak, including a twelve-year-old boy and at least two female civilians, as well as nine soldiers of the KLA. At least one civilian, Nazmi Ymeri (76), was executed in his yard. Witnesses claim that Banush Kamberi, whose headless body was found in his yard, was last seen alive in the custody of the police. At least two people, Bajram Mehmeti and his daughter Hanumshahe (20), were killed by a grenade thrown by the police as they were running through the street.

Human Rights Watch confirmed that a group of approximately forty policeman, in blue uniforms and without masks, shot from a distance of twenty meters on unarmed civilians who were running through their yards. They killed Riza Beqa (44), Zejnel Beqa (22), and Halim Beqa (12), and wounded two women, Zyhra Beqa (42) and her daughter Fetije (18). It is believed that local policemen from the nearby Stimlje police station participated in this action.

The attack on civilians in Račak is one in a long series of war crimes committed by the Yugoslav Army and Serbian police during the Kosovo conflict. Since February 1998, government troops have systematically destroyed civilian property, attacked civilians, and committed summary executions, all of which are grave breaches of the laws of war. The Kosovo Liberation Army (KLA) has also committed some serious abuses, such as the taking of civilian hostages and summary executions (documented in the Human Rights Watch report "Humanitarian Law Violations in Kosovo" available, along with other Kosovo reports, on the web site www.hrw.org). The KLA in the Shtimle and Suva Reka area was particularly known for a high number of kidnappings of ethnic Serbs.

Human Rights Watch called on the Yugoslav government to allow an unhindered investigation by international forensics experts and the war crimes tribunal to determine the precise nature of events. Government authorities, directly implicated in the crime, cannot be trusted to conduct an impartial investigation.

The organization also called on the international community to take resolute action against Yugoslav President Slobodan Milosevic and his government for brazenly violating international humanitarian law. International inaction in the face of past atrocities, the organization said, gave President Milosevic the rightful impression that he could continue his abusive campaign with impunity.

Finally, Human Rights Watch called on the Contact Group to insist that the Chief Prosecutor of the International War Crimes Tribunal for the Former Yugoslavia, Louise Arbour, be granted access to Račak and other sites of atrocities in Kosovo.

HUMAN RIGHTS WATCH REPORT
Yugoslav Government War Crimes in Račak

Background

The village of Račak, about half a kilometer from the town of Stimlje, had a pre-conflict population of approximately 2,000 people. During the large-scale government offensive in August 1998, the Serbian police shelled Račak, and several family compounds were looted and burned. Since then, most of the population has lived in Stimlje or nearby Uroševac. On the day before the January 15 attack, less then four hundred people were in the village. The KLA was also in Račak, with a base near the power plant. A number of ethnic Serbs were kidnapped in the Stimlje region, mostly during the summer.

The January 15 attack might have been provoked by a well-prepared KLA ambush near Dulje (west of Stimlje) on January 8, in which three Serbian policeman were killed and one was wounded. On January 10, the KLA ambushed another police patrol in Slivovo (south of Stimlje), killing one policeman. A Yugoslav Army buildup in the area around Stimlje ensued over the next four days, especially on the mountain road between Dulje and Caraljevo villages.

The Police Action in Račak

Witnesses told Human Rights Watch that they heard automatic weapons fire beginning around 6:30 a.m. on January 15, when the police reportedly exchanged fire with the KLA from a hill called Česta. Half an hour later, army tanks and armored cars came as backup and shelled the forest near the neighboring village of Petrovo, where some KLA units were positioned. They also fired at some family compounds in Račak. Some families managed to escape Račak, fleeing towards Petrovo, which was also affected along with the villages of Malopoljce and Belinca.

Around 7:00 a.m., Račak was surrounded by the Serbian police. Several witnesses told Human Rights Watch that they saw seven blue armored vehicles on Česta hill, as well as three VJ tanks (type T-55). The police were shooting and some heavy artillery was fired directly into some houses near Malopoljce and Petrovo from a position in the nearby forest called, in Albanian, Pishat.

The extent of the fighting in Račak that morning remains somewhat unclear. According to one Serbian policeman, the KLA's resistance around Račak lasted almost four hours, and when they were finally able to enter the village the police confiscated three mounted machine guns. Villagers, however, said that the police had entered the village by 9:00 a.m. They said that there was shooting and some artillery until 4:00 p.m. By 4:30 p.m., the police had left the village.

Deliberate Killings of the Beqa Family Members

Ten households of the Beqa family live in the part of Račak called Upper Mahalla on the edge of the village. According to one member of the family, whose son and husband were both killed, at around 7:00 a.m. thirty members of the Beqa family tried to run toward the nearby forest when they heard the police. She told Human Rights Watch that more then forty policemen wearing blue uniforms and without masks began shooting at them from a distance of twenty meters from the top of the hill. She said:

My son H.B. was running on my left side, maybe two meters from me. He had his trousers in his hands, we did not have time to dress properly. He was warning me to move aside and suddenly he fell down. The bullet hit him in the neck. In front of me my husband fell as well. He didn't move any more.

Another person in the same group, aged seventy, told Human Rights Watch how he saw his twenty-two-year-old grandson shot dead, while his eighteen-year-old granddaughter and her mother were both wounded.

The other members of the Beqa family ran back to a house and hid under the steps until nightfall. Nobody dared to help the wounded, who spent two hours crawling for shelter from the police. One young women said that the police stayed on the hill singing songs and calling her relative by name in the Albanian language ("Aziz, come here to see your dead relatives!"), which suggests that local policemen from Stimlje who were familiar with the residents of Račak may have participated in the attack.

Killed by Grenade

According to M.B., who was hiding in his home, Bajram Mehmeti and his daughter Hanumshahe were killed by a grenade early in the morning of January 15 as they were running through the center of the village. He said:

My cousins were lying twenty meters from the water well. He was hit in the head and she was hit in the chest. One man pulled her in the house and she died in his hands.

Searching for Weapons and the Killing of Nazmi Ymeri (76)

According to eleven different witnesses interviewed separately, groups of about thirty policemen each were entering Račak from different directions beginning around 7:00 a.m. By 9:00 a.m., most of them had gathered in the village center near the mosque. These policemen also wore blue uniforms but they had masks on their faces with slits for their eyes and mouth, and they wore helmets. Some of them had "rocket propelled grenades" strapped to their backs. These police searched house by house, witnesses said, looking for people and weapons. Most of the hidden civilians, upon seeing the police in the village center, ran in the opposite direction towards another part of the village.

One witness, S.A. (46), was hiding with his wife and the five children of his neighbor between the house and stable of Hyrzi Bilalli. From this spot, he said he overheard a discussion held by a group of policemen. He told Human Rights Watch:

I heard clearly when one said, "Release everybody under the age of fifteen. You know what to do with the others." I heard when another one gave the order to pick up the bodies from the yards in plastic bags and put them in the cars. They took away the body of Ahmet's wife who was shot on the street while she was trying to run from one house to another. I later saw the place where her body was. It was just a pool of blood.

The same witness said that the same group of policeman went into the next door house of the elderly Nazmi Imeri, who lived alone, and was later found dead. He said:

I heard shooting and a scream. In the evening I went in his [Imeri's] yard and took his body to our yard. The top of the head was blown off.

Torture in the Yard of Sadik Osmani

As the police were in the Račak, many villager made their way, running and hiding, to the large house of Sadik Osmani near the place called, in Albanian, Kodra e Bebushit. One boy who was present, aged twelve, told Human Rights Watch that approximately thirty men and four boys, himself included, decided to hide in Osmani's stable. A group of approximately twenty women and children hid in the cellar of Osmani's three-storey house. The police later detained, beat, and executed the men in the stable (see below), but the women and children in the cellar were left unharmed.

According to the boy, the police entered Osmani's yard sometime before noon. One tall policeman wearing a black mask and a helmet with a blue police uniform kicked in the door and immediately began to shoot over the heads of the thirty men lying on the ground, who were screaming "Don't shoot! We are civilians!"

All of the men were taken outside into the yard, where they were forced to lie on the ground and searched for weapons. The four boys were taken out of this group, including the twelve-year-old who spoke with Human Rights Watch, and were locked up together with the women and other children in Osmani's cellar. The police also took four men from the cellar — Sadik Osmani, Burim Osmani, Rama Shabani, and Mufail Hajrizi — and put them with the other men in the yard. Burim Osmani, who is a teenager around fifteen years old, was later put back into the cellar, apparently because he was too young. The conscious decision to return him, while later executing the others, suggests that the police had a clear order to kill the adult males of the village.

Before the twelve-year-old boy was sent to the cellar, however, he saw how the police beat the men in the yard, including his father and some other relatives. The boy told Human Rights Watch:

Two or three policeman beat them with wooden sticks. One was kicking them in the face with his boots. The others were just watching. It was terrible. The men were screaming, and their heads were covered with blood. A policeman locked me in the cellar with the women, but I could hear screaming for the next half an hour.

This version of events was corroborated by three other women locked in the cellar who spoke with Human Rights Watch in two separate interviews, although they could not see the men in the yard. All of them believed that the police had only arrested their male relatives and taken them away to the police station in Stimlje. It was only the next day when they realized that the twenty-three men had been killed.

Extrajudicial Executions

Some time around 1:00 p.m. the police led the twenty-three men out of Osmani's yard. One witness, S. A., was hidden at that time behind a compound wall fifty meters from the Osmani house. He told Human Rights Watch that he heard the police leading the detained men through the Račak streets. He said:

> I heard the police ask them [the men] where is the headquarters of our army [the KLA], and they answered where it was. Then they went together toward the power station in the direction of our army. I think it was maybe 3:00 p.m. when I heard shooting, but I did not know that they were killed.

Members of the OSCE's Kosovo Verification Mission (KVM) entered Račak late in the afternoon of January 15, after having been prevented from entering the area during the day by VJ and police forces. The KVM took five wounded persons, including a woman and a boy suffering from gunshot wounds, and left. During the night, the remaining men of the village searched for the wounded, still thinking that the twenty-three men were in the Stimlje police station. One person who participated in the search told Human Rights Watch that they found the bodies on the hill called Kodri e Bebushit, in Albanian, around 4:00 a.m.. He said:

> I saw Mufail Hajrizi. He was slashed on the chest. Then we found Haqif, the guest from Petrovo. His body was lying on his side with the hands as if he wanted to defend himself. His throat and half his face had been cut by a knife. On the top of his head was a wooden stick with some paper. Something was written on that paper but I can't remember what it was. There were more than twenty bodies, almost all of them were my relatives. We wanted to cover the bodies with blankets, or something else, but one man said not to touch anything before KVM comes tomorrow.

One woman, L.S., told Human Rights Watch that her son and husband had survived the execution. She told Human Rights Watch:

> In the morning I got information that the men from the stable were found dead. But soon I saw my husband and son coming toward me — like they were standing up from the grave. My son told me that the group of policeman had pushed them with their hands behind their heads to go towards the hill. My son was in front with Sadik, and the others were behind. When he came to the top of the hill, he saw another group of policeman waiting for them with rifles. He turned his head and shouted to the others to run away. He ran toward the village of Rance, and didn't turn his head. One bullet crossed through his pocket, and another one is still in his belt.

Precisely how the twenty-three men were killed by the police on the hill outside of Račak remains somewhat unclear. But witness testimony, as provided here, and the physical evidence found at the site by journalists and KVM monitors, makes it clear that most of these men were fired upon from close range as they offered no resistance. Some of them were apparently shot while trying to run away.

Journalists at the scene early on January 16 told Human Rights Watch that many of these twenty-three men also had signs of torture, such as missing finger nails. Their clothes were bloody, with slashes and holes at the same spots as their bullet entry and exits wounds, which argues against government claims that the victims were KLA soldiers who were dressed in civilian clothes after they had been killed. All of them were wearing rubber boots typical of Kosovo farmers rather than military footwear.

It is possible that some of these men were defending their village in the morning and then went to the Osmani house once they saw the police entering the village. However, they clearly did not resist the police at the time of their capture or execution. They were tortured and arbitrarily killed — crimes that can never be justified in times of war or peace.

The Forensic Investigation

After a thorough inspection of the bodies by KVM, villagers collected the bodies and transported them to the Račak mosque. Two days later, however, under heavy arm, the police entered the village and took the corpses to the morgue in Prishtina.

On January 25, head of the Institute of Forensic Medicine in Prishtina, Slavisa Dobricanin, announced that autopsies had been conducted on twenty-one bodies, some of them conducted in the presence of OSCE personnel. None of the bodies bore the signs of a massacre, he said. The OSCE did not comment on its impressions of the procedures or the announced results.

A Finnish pathology team subsequently took over for the OSCE, and began to participate in the autopsy procedures together with the government authorities. The team distanced itself from Dobricanin's statements and, on January 26, expressed concern that there had been a tampering with the evidence, although they did not clarify by whom or when. The results of the Finns' investigations should be made public in early February.

The International War Crimes Tribunal for the Former Yugoslavia (ICTY)

Human rights organizations can document the abuses taking place in Kosovo, and the international community can take steps to bring these abuses to an end. But only one institution has been entrusted by the international community to prosecute the persons responsible for violations of humanitarian law: the International Criminal Tribunal for the Former Yugoslavia (ICTY). The role of the ICTY is of crucial importance, as the prosecution of those who commit atrocities is likely to have a significant deterrence effect in addition to upholding the principles of international justice.

ICTY's jurisdiction over war crimes committed in Kosovo is indisputable under the mandate established by U.N. Security Council resolution 827, and has been repeatedly reaffirmed by the U.N. Security Council in its resolutions on Kosovo, as well as by the tribunal itself. In the absence of any efforts on the part of Yugoslav authorities to bring the perpetrators of humanitarian law violations to justice, the ICTY represents the only avenue to prosecute abusers.

The Yugoslav authorities have consistently refused to accept the jurisdiction of the ICTY, and have frustrated the work of ICTY investigators in Kosovo by denying them visas and barring them from carrying out investigations. Only a few ICTY investigators have been able to gain access to Kosovo, and even they have been officially prohibited by the Yugoslav authorities from interviewing persons or gathering evidence. The Yugoslav authorities base their refusal to cooperate with the ICTY on their view that the conflict in Kosovo is an internal dispute with "terrorists," a view repeatedly rejected by the ICTY, the U.N. Security Council, and other international actors, including Human Rights Watch.

On January 18, Chief Prosecutor of the ICTY, Louise Arbour, attempted to enter Kosovo through Macedonia in order to "investigate the reported atrocities in Račak." She did not have a Yugoslav visa, having been denied one by the authorities, and was refused entry into the country. Back in The Hague, Arbour stated unequivocally that she will be investigating the massacre in Račak "with or without access to the territory." Regarding the fears of evidence tampering, she said:

> Evidence of tampering — should such evidence become available, is, in fact, excellent circumstantial evidence of guilt. If one can trace where the order to tamper came from, it permits a pretty strong inference that it was done for the purpose of hiding the truth, which demonstrates consciences of guilt.

Western governments and the Contact Group, including Russia, have called on President Milosevic to cooperate with the ICTY. More than just a visa for Arbour, this should mean unrestricted access for ICTY's investigators to Račak and the sites of other humanitarian law violations in Kosovo committed by both the KLA and the government.

IX. APPENDIX B: LEGAL STANDARDS AND THE KOSOVO CONFLICT

International Law

Until 1998, human rights abuses in Kosovo, as documented in numerous human rights reports,[113] were evaluated against the norms of international human rights law. Police abuse, arbitrary arrests, and violations of due process constituted violations of, among other instruments, the Universal Declaration of Human Rights and the International Covenant on Civil and Political Rights, which the Yugoslav government has pledged to respect.[114]

The growth of armed opposition by the UÇK, however, and the intensification of fighting between government forces and this armed insurgency, have altered the nature of the conflict in Kosovo. Since February, intense fighting has resulted in an estimated six hundred deaths and the displacement of 300,000 persons, while hundreds of villages have been destroyed. Documented abuses include extrajudicial executions, the use of disproportionate force, indiscriminate attacks against civilians, and the systematic destruction of civilian property by the Serbian special police and Yugoslav Army, as well as abuses, such as hostage taking and summary executions, committed against Serbian and Albanian civilians by the UÇK.

By all estimations, the Yugoslav government is fighting against an armed insurgency that has waged ongoing and concerted attacks against the Serbian police and Yugoslav Army, and has controlled large sections of Kosovo, albeit temporarily. In terms of international law, the confrontation is considered an "armed conflict."

The conduct of both government forces and the armed insurgency in an armed conflict is governed by international humanitarian law, known as the rules of war, and in particular Article 3 common to the four 1949 Geneva Conventions, Protocol II to those conventions, and the customary laws of war.[115] Like human

---

[113]Human Rights Watch reports include: *Increasing Turbulence: Human Rights in Yugoslavia*, October 1989; *Yugoslavia: Crisis in Kosovo*, with the International Helsinki Federation, March 1990; *Yugoslavia: Human Rights Abuses in Kosovo 1990-1992*, October 1992; *Open Wounds: Human Rights Abuses in Kosovo*, March 1993; *Persecution Persists: Human Rights Violations in Kosovo*, December 1996.

[114]Yugoslavia ratified the International Covenant on Civil and Political Rights on June 2, 1971.

[115]Yugoslavia acceded to the four Geneva Conventions on April 21, 1950, and to Protocols I and II on June 11, 1979.

rights law, humanitarian law prohibits summary executions, torture, and other inhuman treatment and the application of ex post facto law. The essential difference is that the provisions of humanitarian law that apply in times of armed conflict are not derogable nor capable of suspension.

The special significance of the Kosovo situation having passed the threshold of an "armed conflict" is that it invokes the jurisdiction of the International Criminal Tribunal for the Former Yugoslavia, which is mandated to prosecute intra alia crimes against humanity and violations of the laws or customs of war in the territory of the former Yugoslavia.[116]

Kosovo as an Internal Armed Conflict

International humanitarian law makes a critical distinction between international and non-international (internal) armed conflicts, and a proper characterization of the conflict is important to determine which aspects of international humanitarian law apply. Article 2 common to the four Geneva Conventions of 1949 states that an international armed conflict must involve a declared war or any other armed conflict which may arise "between two or more of the High Contracting Parties" to the convention. The official commentary to the 1949 Geneva Conventions broadly defines "armed conflict" as any difference between two states leading to the intervention of armed forces.[117]

---

[116]On July 7, 1998, the Tribunal declared publicly that the hostilities in Kosovo had reached the level of an armed conflict, although the starting date for this designation was not stated. In a letter to members of the Contact Group dealing with the Kosovo crisis, Justice Louise Arbour declared:

> [T]he nature and scale of the fighting indicate that an "armed conflict",
> within the meaning of international law, exists in Kosovo. As a
> consequence, she intends to bring charges for crimes against humanity
> or war crimes, if evidence of such crimes is established.

The U.S. government has a similar position. On August 31, U.S. ambassador-at-large for war crimes issues, David Scheffer, said, "there is no question that an armed conflict exists in Kosovo. There is also no question that the War Crimes Tribunal has jurisdiction to investigate and prosecute war crimes and crimes against humanity committed in Kosovo pursuant to U.N. Security Council Resolution 827 (1993), which covers the former Yugoslavia."

[117]International Committee of the Red Cross, *Commentary*, III Geneva Convention (International Committee of the Red Cross: Geneva 1960), p. 23.

An internal armed conflict is more difficult to define, since it is sometimes debatable whether hostilities within a state have reached the level of an armed conflict, in contrast to tensions, disturbance, riots, or isolated acts of violence. The official commentary to Common Article 3 of the Geneva Conventions, which regulates internal armed conflicts, lists a series of conditions that, although not obligatory, provide some convenient guidelines. First and foremost among these is whether the party in revolt against the de jure government, in this case the UÇK, "possesses an organized military force, an authority responsible for its acts, acting within a determinate territory and having the means of respecting and ensuring respect for the Convention."[118]

Other conditions outlined in the convention's commentary deal with the government's response to the insurgency. Another indication that there is an internal armed conflict is the government's recognition that it is obliged to use its regular military forces against an insurgency.[119]

Internal armed conflicts that reach a higher level of hostilities are governed by the 1977 Protocol II to the Geneva Conventions, which is more encompassing than Common Article 3 in its protection of civilians (see below). Protocol II is invoked when armed conflicts:

> [T]ake place in the territory of a High Contracting Party between its armed forces and dissident armed forces or other organized armed groups which, under responsible command, exercise such control over a part of its territory as to enable them to carry out sustained and concerted military operations and to implement this Protocol.[120]

Finally, internal armed conflicts are also governed by customary international law, such as United Nations General Assembly 2444.[121] This resolution, adopted by unanimous vote on December 19, 1969, expressly recognized the customary law principle of civilian immunity and its complementary principle requiring the warring parties to distinguish civilians from

---

[118]International Committee of the Red Cross, *Commentary*, IV Geneva Convention (International Committee of the Red Cross: Geneva 1958), p. 35.

[119]Ibid.

[120]International Committee of the Red Cross Commentary to Protocol II, p. 90.

[121]U.N. General Assembly, *Respect for Human Rights in Armed Conflicts*, United Nations Resolution 2444, G.A. Res. 2444, 23 U.N. GAOR Supp. (No. 18) U.N. Doc. A/7433 (New York: U.N., 1968), p. 164.

combatants at all times. The preamble to this resolution states that these fundamental humanitarian law principles apply "in all armed conflicts," meaning both international and internal armed conflicts.[122] Interpreting its jurisdiction over violations of customs of war committed in the territory of the former Yugoslavia, the ICTY has held that this jurisdiction includes "violations of Common Article 3 and other customary rules on internal conflict" and "violations of agreements binding upon the parties to the conflict, considered qua treaty law, i.e. agreements which have not turned into customary international law" (e.g. Protocol II to the Geneva Convention).[123]

The Applicability of Common Article 3 and Protocol II to the Conflict in Kosovo

The hostilities between the UÇK and government forces had, by February 28, 1998, reached a level of conflict to which the obligations of Common Article 3 apply. Given the subsequent intensity of the conflict from March to September, Human Rights Watch is also evaluating the conduct of the UÇK and government forces based on the standards enshrined in Protocol II to the Geneva Convention.[124]

On February 28, Serbian special police forces launched their first large-scale, military attack on villages — Likošane and Ćirez— suspected of harboring UÇK members. Since that date, the UÇK and the government have been engaged in ongoing hostilities involving military offensives, front lines, and the use of attack helicopters and heavy artillery (mostly by the government). The UÇK possesses small arms and light artillery.

Although the UÇK is primarily a guerilla army with no ridged hierarchical structure, and there are separate internal factions, during the period covered by this

---

[122]U.N. General Assembly Resolution 2444 affirms:

... the following principles for observance by all government and other authorities responsible for action in armed conflicts:

(a)	That the right of the parties to a conflict to adopt means of injuring the enemy is not unlimited;
(b)	That it is prohibited to launch attacks against the civilian populations as such;
©	That distinction must be made at all times between persons taking part in the hostilities and members of the civilian population to the effect that the latter be spared as much as possible.

[123]The Prosecution v. Duško Tadić, Appeals Chamber Decision on the Defense Motion for Interlocutory Appeal on Jurisdiction, para. 89 (October 2, 1995).

[124]Human Rights Watch also takes some concepts from Protocol I, since it provides useful guidance on the rules of war.

report (from February to September) the UÇK was an organized military force for purposes of international humanitarian law. According to those close to the UÇK who were interviewed by Human Rights Watch, at least until the summer offensive by the Serbian special police and Yugoslav Army, the UÇK is believed to have had five or six "operative zones," each with a regional and several subregional commanders. Not all, but most of the regional commanders were represented in the High Command, the body within the UÇK that makes decisions for the whole UÇK. This structure allowed decisions to be transmitted down to the fighters.

Seasoned war correspondents, as well as Human Rights Watch researchers who encountered the UÇK, observed instances of discipline among UÇK fighters manning checkpoints and their tendency to apply similar policies and procedures (for example, with regard to granting journalists access to areas under UÇK control). Such discipline is an indication that the fighters were receiving orders regarding policy and that the fighters were answerable at least to regional commanders. There are also cases, however, when a clear lack of discipline was observed, which points to some structural weaknesses within the UÇK. Despite this, it is clear that the UÇK leadership was able to organize systematic attacks throughout large parts of Kosovo. It also coordinated logistical and financial support from the Albanian diaspora in Western Europe and the United States. Until the Yugoslav Army sealed the border with Albania, arms flowed regularly from Albania's north.

From April until mid-July, 1998, the UÇK held as much as 40 percent of the territory of Kosovo, although most of that territory was retaken by government forces by August 1998. Until then, however, the UÇK had held a number of strategic towns and villages, and manned checkpoints along some of Kosovo's important roads; today their area of control has been reduced to some parts of Drenica and a few scattered pockets in the west, especially at night.

It appears that its command structure has been damaged as a result of the offensive, although it is believed that the nucleus of the organization continues to exist. Complicating the matter is the recent rise of a separate armed Albanian organization known as FARK (Forcat Armatosur e Republikes se Kosoves -- Armed Forces of the Republic of Kosova), which has a separate base in Northern Albania and is mostly present in the Metohija (Dukagjin in Albanian) region of Kosovo. By September 1998, it was clear that this alternative group, comprised mostly of ethnic Albanians with past experience in the Yugoslav Army and police, did not agree with the UÇK's military strategy, criticizing its lack of professionalism. FARK, however, apparently did not exist as an organized force until August 1998.[125]

In interviews and public statements, UÇK spokesmen have also repeatedly expressed the organization's willingness to respect the rules of war, which is one of the factors to be considered in determining whether an internal armed conflict exists.[126] In an interview given to the Albanian-language newspaper *Koha Ditore* in July 1998, UÇK spokesman Jakup Krasniqi said:

> From the start, we had our own internal rules for our operations. These clearly lay down that the UÇK recognizes the Geneva Conventions and the conventions governing the conduct of war.[127]

UÇK Communique number 51, issued by "UÇK General Headquarters" on August 26, stated that, " The UÇK is an institutionalized and organized Army, is getting increasingly professional and ready to fight to victory."[128]

There are reported cases of UÇK soldiers being disciplined by their own commanders for having harassed or shot at foreign journalists, although it is unknown if any UÇK combatants have been punished for targeting ethnic Serb civilians, abusing those in detention, or any other violation of Common Article 3 or Protocol II. Over 100 people, mostly ethnic Serbs, are believed to have been detained by the UÇK.

Finally, through its words and actions, the Yugoslav government has clearly recognized the UÇK as an organized armed force. In addition to the special

---

[125]The ICRC *Commentary* to Article 1 of Protocol II addresses the requirements for control over territory. Paragraph 3.3. says: "In many conflicts there is considerable movement in the theater of hostilities; it often happens that territorial control changes hands rapidly. Sometimes domination of a territory will be relative, for example, when urban centres remain in government hands while rural areas escape their authority. In practical terms, if the insurgent armed groups are organized in accordance with the requirements of the Protocol, the extent of territory they can claim to control will be that which escapes the control of the government armed forces. However, there must be some degree of stability in the control of even a modest area of land for them to be capable of effectively applying the rules of the Protocol."

[126]The ICRC *Commentary* on Common Article 3, paragraph 1, states that an internal armed conflict exists when, "the insurgent civil authority agrees to be bound by the provisions of the Convention."

[127]*Koha Ditore*, July 12, 1998.

[128]UÇK Communique Nr. 51, as published in *Koha Ditore*, August 26, 1998.

police forces, which operate similar to a military organization, the government has been obliged to use regular military forces, the Yugoslav Army, against the insurgents.

The major government offensive that began in July has severely affected the capacity of the UÇK, and may ultimately affect the status of the conflict under the laws of war. However, the conditions of Article 3 and Protocol II were satisfied during the period under the purview of this report (February - August, 1998). Human Rights Watch is, therefore, evaluating the conduct of both the government and the UÇK based on the principles outlined in Common Article 3 and Protocol II.

Common Article 3 and the Protection of Non-combatants

Article 3 common to the four Geneva Conventions has been called a convention within a convention. It is the only provision of the Geneva Conventions that directly applies to internal (as opposed to international) armed conflicts.

Common Article 3, Section 1, states:

In the case of armed conflict not of an international character occurring in the territory of one of the High Contracting Parties, each Party to the conflict shall be bound to apply, as a minimum, the following provisions:

1.   Persons taking no active part in the hostilities, including members of armed forces who had laid down their arms and those placed *hors de combat* by sickness, wounds, detention, or any other cause, shall in all circumstances be treated humanely, without any adverse distinction founded on race, colour, religion or faith, sex, birth or wealth, or any other similar criteria.

To this end the following acts are and shall remain prohibited at any time and in any place whatsoever with respect to the above-mentioned persons:

a.   violence to life and person, in particular murder of all kinds, mutilation, cruel treatment and torture;

b.   taking of hostages;

c.   outrages upon personal dignity, in particular humiliating and degrading treatment;

d.   the passing of sentences and the carrying out of executions without previous judgment pronounced by a regularly constituted court, affording all the judicial guarantees which are recognized as indispensable by civilized peoples.

Common Article 3 thus imposes fixed legal obligations on the parties to an internal armed conflict to ensure humane treatment of persons not, or no longer, taking an active role in the hostilities.

Common Article 3 applies when a situation of internal armed conflict objectively exists in the territory of a State Party; it expressly binds all parties to the internal conflict, including insurgents, although they do not have the legal capacity to sign the Geneva Conventions. In Yugoslavia, the government and the UÇK forces are parties to the conflict and therefore bound by Common Article 3's provisions.

The obligation to apply Article 3 is absolute for all parties to the conflict and independent of the obligation of the other parties. That means that the Yugoslav government cannot excuse itself from complying with Article 3 on the grounds that the UÇK is violating Article 3, and vice versa.

Application of Article 3 by the government cannot be legally construed as recognition of the insurgent party's belligerence, from which recognition of additional legal obligations beyond Common Article 3, would flow. Nor is it necessary for any government to recognize the UÇK's belligerent status for Article 3 to apply.

In contrast to international conflicts, the law governing internal armed conflicts does not recognize the combatant's privilege[129] and therefore does not provide any special status for combatants, even when captured. Thus, the Yugoslav government is not obliged to grant captured members of the UÇK prisoner of war status. Similarly, government army combatants who are captured by the UÇK need

---

[129]The "combatant's privilege" is a license to kill or capture enemy troops, destroy military objectives and cause unavoidable civilian casualties. This privilege immunizes combatants from criminal prosecution by their captors for their violent acts that do not violate the laws of war but would otherwise be crimes under domestic law. Prisoner of war status depends on and flows from this privilege. *See* Solf, "The Status of Combatants in Non-International Armed Conflicts Under Domestic Law and Transnational Practice," *American University Law Review,* No. 33 (1953), p. 59.

not be accorded this status. Any party can agree to treat its captives as prisoners of war, however.

Since the UÇK forces are not privileged combatants, they may be tried and punished by the Yugoslav courts for treason, sedition, and the commission of other crimes under domestic laws.

Protocol II and the Protection of Non-combatants

Protocol II supplements Common Article 3 and provides a more encompassing list of protections for civilians in internal armed conflicts. While not an all-inclusive list, the following practices, orders, and actions are prohibited:

- Orders that there shall be no survivors, such threats to combatants, or direction to conduct hostilities on this basis.

- Acts of violence against all persons, including combatants who are captured, surrender, or are placed *hors de combat*.

- Torture, any form of corporal punishment, or other cruel treatment of persons under any circumstances.

- Pillage and destruction of civilian property. This prohibition is designed to spare civilians the suffering resulting from the destruction of their real and personal property: houses, furniture, clothing, provisions, tools, and so forth. Pillage includes organized acts as well as individual acts without the consent of the military authorities.[130]

- Hostage taking.[131]

---

[130]International Committee of the Red Cross (ICRC), *Commentary, IV Geneva Convention* (Geneva: ICRC, 1958), p.226.

[131]The ICRC *Commentary on the Additional Protocols*, p. 874, defines hostages as

persons who find themselves, willingly or unwillingly, in the power of the enemy and who answer with their freedom or their life for compliance with the orders of the latter and for upholding the security of its armed forces.

- Desecration of corpses.[132] Mutilation of the dead is never permissible and violates the rules of war.

Protocol II also states that children should be provided with care and aid as required. Article 4, paragraph 3 states that no children under the age of fifteen shall be "recruited by the armed forces or groups."

Protection of the Civilian Population

In situations of internal armed conflict, generally speaking, a civilian is anyone who is not a member of the armed forces or of an organized armed group of a party to the conflict. Accordingly, "the civilian population comprises all persons who do not actively participate in the hostilities."[133]

Civilians may not be subject to deliberate individualized attack since they pose no immediate threat to the adversary.[134]

The term "civilian" also includes some employees of the military establishment who are not members of the armed forces but assist them.[135] While as civilians they may not be targeted, these civilian employees of military establishments or those who indirectly assist combatants assume the risk of death or injury incidental to attacks against legitimate military targets while they are at or in the immediate vicinity of military targets.

In addition, both sides may utilize as combatants persons who are otherwise engaged in civilian occupations. These civilians lose their immunity from

---

[132]Protocol II, article 8, states:

Whenever circumstances permit, and particularly after an engagement, all possible measures shall be taken, without delay, . . . to search for the dead, prevent their being despoiled, and decently dispose of them.

[133]R. Goldman, "International Humanitarian Law and the Armed Conflicts in El Salvador and Nicaragua," *American University Journal of International Law and Policy,* Vol. 2 (1987), p. 553.

[134]M. Bothe, K. Partsch, & W. Solf, *New Rules for Victims of Armed Conflicts: Commentary on the Two 1977 Protocols Additional to the Geneva Conventions of 1949* (The Hague: Martinus Nijhoff, 1982), p. 303.

[135]Civilians include those persons who are "directly linked to the armed forces, including those who accompany the armed forces without being members thereof, such as civilian members of military aircraft crews, supply contractors, members of labour units, or of services responsible for the welfare of the armed forces, members of the crew of the merchant marine and the crews of civil aircraft employed in the transportation of military personnel, material or supplies. . . . Civilians employed in the production, distribution and storage of munitions of war. . . ." Ibid., pp. 293-94.

attack for as long as they directly participate in hostilities.[136] "[D]irect participation [in hostilities] means acts of war which by their nature and purpose are likely to cause actual harm to the personnel and equipment of enemy armed forces," and includes acts of defense.[137]

"Hostilities" not only covers the time when the civilian actually makes use of a weapon but also the time that he is carrying it, as well as situations in which he undertakes hostile acts without using a weapon.[138] Examples are provided in the United States Army Field Manual which lists some hostile acts as including:

> sabotage, destruction of communication facilities, intentional misleading of troops by guides, and liberation of prisoners of war. . . . This is also the case of a person acting as a member of a weapons crew, or one providing target information for weapon systems intended for immediate use against the enemy such as artillery spotters or members of ground observer teams. [It] would include direct logistic support for units engaged directly in battle such as the delivery of ammunition to a firing position. On the other hand civilians providing only indirect support to the armed forces, such as workers in defense plants or those engaged in distribution or storage of military supplies in rear areas, do not pose an immediate threat to the adversary and therefore would not be subject to deliberate individual attack.[139]

Persons protected by Common Article 3 include members of both government and UÇK forces who surrender, are wounded, sick or unarmed, or are captured. They are *hors de combat*, literally, out of combat.

Designation of Military Objectives

Under the laws of war, military objectives are defined only as they relate to objects or targets, rather than to personnel. To constitute a legitimate military objective, the object or target, selected by its nature, location, purpose, or use, must contribute effectively to the enemy's military capability or activity, and its total or

---

[136]Ibid., p. 303.
[137]ICRC, *Commentary on the Additional Protocols*, p. 619.
[138]ICRC, *Commentary on the Additional Protocols*, p. 618-19. This is a broader definition than "attacks" and includes at a minimum preparation for combat and return from combat. Bothe, *New Rules for Victims of Armed Conflicts*, p. 303.
[139]Ibid., p. 303 (footnote omitted).

partial destruction or neutralization must offer a definite military advantage in the circumstances.[140]

Legitimate military objectives are combatants' weapons, convoys, installations, and supplies. In addition:

> an object generally used for civilian purposes, such as a dwelling, a bus, a fleet of taxicabs, or a civilian airfield or railroad siding, can become a military objective if its location or use meets [the criteria in Protocol I, art. 52(2)].[141]

Full-time members of the Yugoslav government's armed forces and UÇK combatants are legitimate military targets and subject to attack, individually or collectively, until such time as they become hors de combat, that is, surrender or are wounded or captured.[142]

Policemen without combat duties are not in principle legitimate military targets, nor are certain other government personnel authorized to bear arms such as customs agents.[143] Policemen with combat duties, however, would be proper military targets, subject to direct individualized attack.

Prohibition of Indiscriminate Attacks: The Principle of Proportionality

The civilian population and individual civilians generally are to be protected against attack.

As set out above, to constitute a legitimate military object, the target must 1) contribute effectively to the enemy's military capability or activity, and 2) its total or partial destruction or neutralization must offer a definite military advantage in the circumstances.

The laws of war characterize all objects as civilian unless they satisfy this two-fold test. Objects normally dedicated to civilian use, such as churches, houses and schools, are presumed not to be military objectives. If they in fact do assist the

---

[140]Protocol I, art. 52 (2).

[141]Bothe, *New Rules for Victims of Armed Conflicts*, pp. 306-07.

[142]A wounded or captured combatant is "out of the fighting," and so must be protected.

[143]Report of Working Group B, Committee I, 18 March 1975 (CDDH/I/238/Rev.1; X, 93), in Howard S. Levie, ed., *The Law of Non International Armed Conflict*, (Dordrecht, Netherlands: Martinus Nijhoff, 1987), p. 67. *See* Rosario Conde, "Policemen without Combat Duties: Illegitimate Targets of Direct Attack under Humanitarian Law," student paper (New York: Columbia Law School, May 12, 1989).

enemy's military action, they can lose their immunity from direct attack. This presumption attaches, however, only to objects that ordinarily have no significant military use or purpose. For example, this presumption would not include objects such as transportation and communications systems that under applicable criteria are military objectives.

The attacker also must do everything "feasible" to verify that the objectives to be attacked are not civilian. "Feasible" means "that which is practical or practically possible taking into account all the circumstances at the time, including those relevant to the success of military operations."[144]

Even attacks on legitimate military targets, however, are limited by the principle of proportionality. This principle places a duty on combatants to choose means of attack that avoid or minimize damage to civilians. In particular, the attacker should refrain from launching an attack if the expected civilian casualties would outweigh the importance of the military target to the attacker. The principle of proportionality is codified in Protocol I, Article 51 (5):

> Among others, the following types of attacks are to be considered as indiscriminate: . . .
>
> (b)   an attack which may be expected to cause incidental
>   loss of civilian life, injury to civilians, damage to
>   civilian objects, or a combination thereof, which would
>   be excessive in relation to the concrete and direct
>   military advantage anticipated.

If an attack can be expected to cause incidental civilian casualties or damage, two requirements must be met before that attack is launched. First, there must be an anticipated "concrete and direct" military advantage. "Direct" means "without intervening condition of agency . . . A remote advantage to be gained at some unknown time in the future would not be a proper consideration to weigh against civilian losses."[145]

Creating conditions "conducive to surrender by means of attacks which incidentally harm the civilian population"[146] is too remote and insufficiently military to qualify as a "concrete and direct" military advantage. "A military

---

[144]Bothe, *New Rules for Victims of Armed Conflict*, p. 362 (footnote omitted).
[145]*Ibid.*, p. 365.
[146]ICRC, *Commentary on the Additional Protocols*, p. 685.

advantage can only consist in ground gained and in annihilating or weakening the enemy armed forces."[147]

The second requirement of the principle of proportionality is that the foreseeable injury to civilians and damage to civilian objects not be disproportionate, that is, "excessive" in comparison to the expected "concrete and definite military advantage."

Excessive damage is a relative concept. For instance, the presence of a soldier on leave cannot serve as a justification to destroy the entire village. If the destruction of a bridge is of paramount importance for the occupation of a strategic zone, "it is understood that some houses may be hit, but not that a whole urban area be leveled."[148] There is never a justification for excessive civilian casualties, no matter how valuable the military target.[149]

Indiscriminate attacks are defined in Protocol I, Article 51 (4), as:

a) those which are not directed at a specific military objective;
b) those which employ a method or means of combat which cannot be directed at a specific military objective; or
c) those which employ a method or means of combat the effects of which cannot be limited as required by this Protocol; and consequently, in each such case, are of a nature to strike military objectives and civilians or civilian objects without distinction.

The Protection of Civilians from Displacement

There are only two exceptions to the prohibition on displacement, for war-related reasons, of civilians: their security or imperative military reasons. Article 17 of Protocol II states:

1. The displacement of the civilian population shall not be ordered for reasons related to the conflict unless the security of the civilians involved or imperative military reasons so demand. Should such displacements have to be carried out, all possible

---

[147]Ibid., p. 685. As set out above, to constitute a legitimate military objective, the object, selected by its nature, location, purpose or use must contribute effectively to the enemy's military capability or activity, and its total or partial destruction or neutralization must offer a "definite" military advantage in the circumstances. See Protocol I, art. 52 (2) where this definition is codified.

[148]ICRC, *Commentary on the Additional Protocols*, p. 684.

[149]Ibid., p. 626.

measures shall be taken in order that the civilian population may
be received under satisfactory conditions of shelter, hygiene,
health, safety and nutrition.

The term "imperative military reasons" usually refers to evacuation
because of imminent military operations. The provisional measure of evacuation
is appropriate if an area is in danger as a result of military operations or is liable to
be subjected to intense bombing. It may also be permitted when the presence of
protected persons in an area hampers military operations. The prompt return of the
evacuees to their homes is required as soon as hostilities in the area have ceased.
The evacuating authority bears the burden of proving that its forcible relocation
conforms to these conditions.

Displacement or capture of civilians solely to deny a social base to the
enemy has nothing to do with the security of the civilians. Nor is it justified by
"imperative military reasons," which require "the most meticulous assessment of
the circumstances"[150] because such reasons are so capable of abuse. As the
commentary to Protocol II states:

Clearly, imperative military reasons cannot be justified by
political motives. For example, it would be prohibited to move
a population in order to exercise more effective control over a
dissident ethnic group.[151]

Mass relocation or displacement of civilians for the purpose of denying a willing
social base to the opposing force is prohibited as it responds to such a wholly
political motive.

Even if the government were to show that the displacement were
necessary, it still has the independent obligation to take "all possible measures" to
receive the civilian population "under satisfactory conditions of shelter, hygiene,
health, safety, and nutrition."

Starvation of Civilians as a Method of Combat

Starvation of civilians as a method of combat has become illegal as a
matter of customary international law, as reflected in Protocol II:

---

[150]Ibid., p. 1472.
[151]Ibid.

Article 14 -- Protection of objects indispensable to the survival of the civilian population

Starvation of civilians as a method of combat is prohibited. It is therefore prohibited to attack, destroy, remove or render useless, for that purpose, objects indispensable to the survival of the civilian population, such as foodstuffs, agricultural areas for the production of foodstuffs, crops, livestock, drinking water installations and supplies and irrigation works.

What is prohibited is using starvation as "a weapon to annihilate or weaken the population." Using starvation as a method of warfare does not mean that the population has to reach the point of starving to death before a violation can be proved. What is forbidden is deliberately "causing the population to suffer hunger, particularly by depriving it of its sources of food or of supplies."

This prohibition on starving civilians "is a rule from which no derogation may be made."[152] No exception is allowed for imperative military necessity, for instance.

Article 14 lists the most usual ways in which starvation is brought about. Specific protection is extended to "objects indispensable to the survival of the civilian population," and a non-exhaustive list of such objects follows: "foodstuffs, agricultural areas for the production of foodstuffs, crops, livestock, drinking water installations and supplies and irrigation works." The article prohibits taking certain destructive actions aimed at these essential supplies, and describes these actions with verbs which are meant to cover all eventualities: "attack, destroy, remove or render useless."

The textual reference to "objects indispensable to the survival of the civilian population" does not distinguish between objects intended for the armed forces and those intended for civilians. Except for the case where supplies are specifically intended as provisions for combatants, it is prohibited to destroy or attack objects indispensable for survival, even if the adversary may benefit from them. The prohibition would be meaningless if one could invoke the argument that members of the government's armed forces or armed opposition might make use of the objects in question.[153]

Attacks on objects used "in direct support of military action" are permissible, however, even if these objects are civilian foodstuffs and other objects

---

[152]Ibid., p. 1456.
[153]Ibid., p. 1458-59.

protected under Article 14. This exception is limited to the immediate zone of actual armed engagements, as is obvious from the examples provided of military objects used in direct support of military action: "bombarding a food-producing area to prevent the army from advancing through it, or attacking a food-storage barn which is being used by the enemy for cover or as an arms depot, etc."[154]

The provisions of Protocol I, Article 54 are also useful as a guideline to the narrowness of the permissible means and methods of attack on foodstuffs.[155] Like Article 14 of Protocol II, Article 54 of Protocol I permits attacks on military food supplies. It specifically limits such attacks to those directed at foodstuffs intended for the sole use of the enemy's armed forces. This means "supplies already in the hands of the adverse party's armed forces because it is only at that point that one could know that they are intended for use only for the members of the enemy's armed forces."[156] Even then, the attacker cannot destroy foodstuffs "in the military supply system intended for the sustenance of prisoners of war, the civilian population of occupied territory or persons classified as civilians serving with, or accompanying, the armed forces."[157]

Proof of Intent to Starve Civilians

Under Article 14, what is forbidden are actions taken with the intention of using starvation as a method or weapon to attack the civilian population. Such an intent may not be easy to prove and most armies will not admit this intent. Proof does not rest solely on the attacker's own statements, however. Intent may be inferred from the totality of the circumstances of the military campaign.

Particularly relevant to assessment of intent is the effort the attacker makes to comply with the duties to distinguish between civilians and military targets and to avoid harming civilians and the civilian economy.[158] If the attacker does not

---

[154]Ibid., p. 657. The *New Rules* gives the following examples of direct support: "an irrigation canal used as part of a defensive position, a water tower used as an observation post, or a cornfield used as cover for the infiltration of an attacking force." Bothe, *New Rules for Victims of Armed Conflicts*, p. 341.

[155]Article 54 of Protocol I is the parallel standard, for international armed conflicts, to Article 14, Protocol II in its prohibition of starvation of civilians as a method of warfare.

[156]Bothe, *New Rules for Victims of Armed Conflict*, p. 340.

[157]Ibid., pp. 340-41.

[158]Civilians are not legitimate military targets; this is also expressly established by U.N. General Assembly Resolution 2444, above. The duty to distinguish at all times between civilians and combatants, and between civilian objects and military objects, includes the duty to direct military operations only against military objectives.

comply with these duties, and food shortages result, an intent to attack civilians by starvation may be inferred.

The more sweeping and indiscriminate the measures taken which result in food shortages, when other less restrictive means of combat are available, the more likely the real intent is to attack the civilian population by depriving it of food. For instance, an attacker who conducts a scorched earth campaign in enemy territory to deprive the enemy of sources of food may be deemed to have an intention of attacking by starvation the civilian population living in enemy territory. The attacker may not claim ignorance of the effects upon civilians of such a scorched earth campaign, since these effects are a matter of common knowledge and publicity. In particular, relief organizations, both domestic and international, usually sound the alarm of impending food shortages occurring during conflicts in order to bring pressure on the parties to permit access for food delivery and to raise money for their complex and costly operations.

The true intentions of the attacker also must be judged by the effort it makes to take prompt remedies, such as permitting relief convoys to reach the needy or itself supplying food to remedy hunger. An attacker who fails to make adequate provision for the affected civilian population, who blocks access to those who would do so, or who refuses to permit civilian evacuation in times of food shortage, may be deemed to have the intent to starve that civilian population.

Domestic Law

The federal constitution of Yugoslavia, promulgated in 1992, established Yugoslavia as a democratic state "founded on the rule of law." The forty-nine articles of the section on rights and freedoms guarantee all Yugoslav citizens basic civil and political rights, such as free speech, free association and the right to a fair trial.

Yugoslav laws guarantee all defendants the right to due process. Article 23 of the federal constitution forbids arbitrary detention and obliges the authorities to inform a detainee immediately of the reason for his or her detention and grant that person access to a lawyer. Article 24 obliges the authorities to inform the detainee in writing of the reason for his or her arrest within twenty-four hours. Detention ordered by a lower court may not exceed three months, unless extended by a higher court to a maximum of six months. Article 25 outlaws torture, as well as any coercion of confessions or statements. The use of force against a detainee is also a criminal offence.

The constitution guarantees the rights of minorities to "preserve, foster and express their ethnic, cultural, linguistic and other attributes, as well as to use their national symbols, in accordance with international law."[159] Article 20 states that:

> Citizens shall be equal irrespective of their nationality, race, sex, language, faith, political or other beliefs, education, social origin, property, or other personal status.

Articles 46 and 47 guarantee minorities the right to education and media in their mother tongue, as well as the right to establish educational and cultural associations. Article 48, however, places some restrictions on free association for minorities. It states:

> Members of national minorities have the right to establish and foster unhindered relations with co-nationals within the Republic of Yugoslavia and outside its borders with co-nationals in other states, and to take part in international nongovernmental organizations, *provided these relations are not detrimental to the Federal Republic of Yugoslavia or to a member republic.* [Emphasis added.]

The Yugoslav constitution also guarantees that the government will respect international law. Article 10 states:

> The Federal Republic of Yugoslavia shall recognize and guarantee the rights and freedoms of man and the citizen recognized under international law.

Article 16 adds:

> The Federal Republic of Yugoslavia shall fulfill in good faith the obligations contained in international treaties to which it is a contracting party. International treaties which have been ratified and promulgated in conformity with the present Constitution and generally accepted rules of international law shall be a constituent part of the internal legal order.

---

[159]Constitution of the Federal Republic of Yugoslavia, Article 11.